Luther Benaiah Wolf

After fifty years

An historical sketch of the Guntur mission of the Evangelical Lutheran Church

Luther Benaiah Wolf

After fifty years
An historical sketch of the Guntur mission of the Evangelical Lutheran Church

ISBN/EAN: 9783337126971

Printed in Europe, USA, Canada, Australia, Japan

Cover: Foto ©ninafisch / pixelio.de

More available books at **www.hansebooks.com**

OR

AN HISTORICAL SKETCH OF THE GUNTUR MISSION OF THE EVANGELICAL LUTHERAN CHURCH OF THE GENERAL SYNOD IN THE UNITED STATES OF AMERICA.

BY

Rev. L. B. WOLF, A. M.,

PRINCIPAL OF THE ARTHUR G. WATTS' MEMORIAL COLLEGE, AND FELLOW OF THE MADRAS UNIVERSITY.

WITH AN INTRODUCTION
BY
REV. E. J. WOLF, D. D.,

PROFESSOR OF CHURCH HISTORY AND N. T. EXEGESIS, THEOLOGICAL SEMINARY, GETTYSBURG, PA.

PUBLISHED FOR THE AUTHOR.

PHILADELPHIA:
LUTHERAN PUBLICATION SOCIETY.

THE AUTHOR'S PREFACE.

In the year 1892, when the celebration of the Jubilee of the Mission was first spoken of, it was determined that one feature of the celebration was to be the publication of an Historical Sketch of the Mission. The task was assigned to the author of this book. It is hardly necessary to state that the work should long ere this have been done, but it is only fair to say that the delay was such as could not be avoided. Effort of this sort, in addition to the claims of a busy missionary life, becomes no slight burden, though in the author's case it was one in which he has had sincere satisfaction. The book aims to give its historical information from first sources, and from the personal experience of over a decade in the field. All foreign terms have as far as possible been avoided, and the spelling of all proper names has not been loaded down with the diacritical points of the scholar, as it is pretty fully recognized that only a residence in the land will enable one to acquire a correct pronunciation of Indian names.

The author's thanks are due to the sainted Dr. C. A. Hay, of Gettysburg, for much of the matter of the opening chapters, and to Dr. Unangst, who has been in active connection with the Mission for over thirty-five years of the time treated of in the following pages, and who has carefully reviewed the manuscript, giving many valuable facts and hints out of his large experience. Nor can the author forget the valuable help rendered by Miss Kistler in furnishing the photographic scenes for the illustrations. Most of them have been taken by her own hand, and will no doubt be most helpful in rendering life-like much that would be otherwise dull and uninteresting.

The hope of the author is that the book may conduce to a more intelligent conception of our Mission and its work among the people of our own dear Church, and awaken a deeper interest and zeal in this great cause of world-evangelization. That such a hope may be realized is his prayer, and with it the book is laid before the Church of whose Mission it treats.

THE AUTHOR.

CONTENTS.

	PAGE
Illustrations, List of	vii
Introduction by Prof. E. J. Wolf, D. D.	xi
Introduction by the Author	15

CHAPTER I.
The Founding of the Missionary Society in America 27

CHAPTER II.
The General Synod's Mission Field 36

CHAPTER III.
Our Field Continued 72

CHAPTER IV.
The Mission's Foreign Staff 80
  Heyer, Gunn, Martz, Grönning, Heise, Snyder, Cutter, Long.

CHAPTER V.
Foreign Staff Continued 122
  Unangst, Harpster, Uhl, Rowe, Schnure, Boggs, Wolf, Kugler, Dryden, Swartz, Nichols, Kistler, Aberly, Sadtler, Albrecht, Yeiser.

CHAPTER VI.
Indian Staff 164
  Early Efforts, Gradual Efficiency, Present Conditions, Future Prospects.

CHAPTER VII.

Organization 181
> Division of the Field and Work, Character of the Work Undertaken by Each, Medical, Zenana.

CHAPTER VIII.

Organization Continued—Educational 203
> General Considerations—Its Place in Missions—Duff's Early Work—Schools in Relation to Government—The Position of Higher Education—Girls' Schools: Early Origin, Present Condition—Mixed or Congregational Schools, Their Work—Boarding Schools, Their Necessity and Aim—High School and College—Mission Colleges, Their Aim—The Development of Our College, Its Position in Our Work.

CHAPTER IX.

Organization Continued—Evangelization 252

CHAPTER X.

Progress 269
> General Considerations — Negative Results — Indian Field only Old Question—Our Mission Progress, Numerical—Mental—Moral—Spiritual.

CHAPTER XI.

Prospects—Conclusions 288

APPENDIX I.

1842-1892. By Rev. L. L. Uhl, Ph.D. Jubilee Tour 293

APPENDIX II.

Rules of the American Evangelical Lutheran Mission 303

ILLUSTRATIONS.

	PAGE
Author's Portrait	Frontispiece
Sacred Bull Idol	37
A Group of Servants	38
Heathen Temple on a Feast Day	40
Four Generations	45
A Muhammadan Woman	46
Group of Elephants	54
Scene in Vinukonda	56
Nichols Memorial Bungalow, Narasarowpet	58
Sub-Collector's Bungalow, Guntur	61
Hindu Temple in Guntur	62
Muhammadan Tomb in Guntur	64
Temple Tower at Bapatla	67
Palmyra Tope (Grove) at Bapatla	68
Rev. C. F. Heyer	89
Rev. and Mrs. Walter Gunn	104
Rev. George J. Martz	109

ILLUSTRATIONS.

	PAGE
Rev. and Mrs. W. E. Snyder	114
Rev. and Mrs. W. I. Cutter	117
Rev. and Mrs. Adam Long	119
Rev. Dr. and Mrs. E. Unangst	123
Rev. E. Unangst, D. D., in His Study	125
Rev. J. H. Harpster, D. D.	127
Rev. and Mrs. L. L. Uhl	130
Rev. and Mrs. A. D. Rowe	132
Rev. A. D. Rowe's Monument, Guntur	139
Rev. and Mrs. Charles Schnure and Miss Kate Boggs	141
Mrs. L. B. Wolf	143
Rev. and Mrs. John Nichols	146
Rev. John Aberly	148
Mrs. John Aberly	149
Rev. Geo. Albrecht	150
Rev. and Mrs. N. E. Yeiser	152
Miss Kate Boggs	156
Miss Anna S. Kugler, M. D.	158
Miss Fannie M. Dryden, B. A.	160
Miss Susan R. Kistler	161
Miss Amy L. Sadtler	162
Sons of Sub-Pastor N. Robert	172
Zenana Home, Guntur	182

ILLUSTRATIONS.

	PAGE
Muhammadan Women at Work in Industrial School	185
A District Bullock Coach	187
A Group of Missionaries	190
Gundingchunam (Plaster) for the New Hospital	192
The Mission Dispensary, Guntur, with Miss Dr. Kugler and Bandy	193
Woman's Hospital, Guntur, (June, 1895)	194
Zenana Ladies and Bible Women	197
Rev. L. B. Wolf, A. M., Principal of Watts' Memorial College, and Teachers	204
Girls' Boarding School, Guntur	212
Hindu Girls' School, Chilakalurupet	214
Miss Minnie Moses, with Normal Class of 1894	215
Samaladas Agraharam—Girls' School	216
Corner-Stone of Arthur G. Watts' Memorial College	243
Arthur G. Watts, M. D., Baltimore, Md., U. S. A., Born January 10, 1861, Died June 10, 1888	244
Lord Wenlock, Governor Madras Presidency, and Staff, Missionaries, Professors and Students, at Opening of the College, March 17, 1893	246
The Arthur G. Watts' Memorial College Building, Approaching Completion	248
The Arthur G. Watts' Memorial College Building at the Formal Opening, March 17, 1893	249
Telugu Congregation, Guntur	273

ILLUSTRATIONS.

	PAGE
A GROUP OF CHRISTIANS, GUNTUR	277
REV. DR. UNANGST AND N. ROBERT, REVISING THE TELUGU BIBLE	278
A GROUP OF CHRISTIANS, GUNTUR	280
A NATIVE CHRISTIAN FEAST, CHRISTMAS DAY	286

ity and progress as is never withheld from those who show their faith in the Head of the Church by using the weapons which He has placed at their disposal.

The founding of this Mission is of course traced to its weak but earnest beginning in the bosom of the Lutheran Church of this country, and the varying fidelity and wisdom and support which the parent has for half a century bestowed upon this child are presented, as might be expected from a true son of the Church, with the hand of Shem rather than with that of Ham.

The author shows throughout these pages an admirable capacity for recognizing the extent of serious, inevitable and stubborn obstacles encountered by missions in pagan lands. His zeal for the work has not blinded him to its difficulties. His conscience, too, holds him by a firmer grip than his enthusiasm; and while optimistic in temper and serenely confident of the ultimate victory, he not only gives a complete survey of the field with its multitudinous and complex hindrances, but he also takes pains to describe things as they actually are, rather than as he and his readers would fain have them.

He is no more of a theorizer than an enthusiast. He grapples the real situation of things without drawing on the imagination, and while clearly understanding current objections to certain methods and policies, he does not resort to special pleading, but cites the facts, which are more reliable than the figures, to testify as to the validity and force of such criticisms, when brought face to face with the whole scope of missionary endeavor, whose aim it is to touch human life at every point and to gain for the ages the ascendency of Christianity over the entire domain of society.

The reader need not expect to have his emotions played upon by thrilling dramatic narrative, nor to have kindled within him those fires of enthusiasm which are wont to be extinguished with the laying down of a glowing volume; but he will find himself entertained, instructed, edified, by a sober, intelligent and intelligible survey of the past fortunes of the Mission maintained in India by the Lutheran Church in America, and of its present complex but magnificent organization. And the moderation and discrimination observed by the writer, and the manifest sincerity of his aim at accuracy and fidelity of statement, must confirm the reader's confidence as he completes chapter after chapter, and in the same degree increase his interest in the sober, truthful narrative.

The historical and biographical matter cannot fail to touch many hearts. Whatever may be, or may not be, the sacrifices demanded of missionaries to-day, those of fifty and forty years ago here recounted, show a measure of devotion, of self-abnegation, and of heroism, in which a church capable of producing such examples of faith may take a just pride. But it is to be hoped also that those who glory in this noble record will take to heart the powerful lesson which it inculcates, and that through these brave confessors the whole Church will be brought to the high and holy resolve to be "dedicated to the unfinished work that they have thus far so nobly carried on." In the immortal words of the illustrious martyr for his country, it is meet "that from these honored dead we take increased devotion to the cause for which they gave the last full measure of devotion, and that we highly resolve that these dead," whose ashes are mingling with the soil of India, "shall not have died in vain."

The wide reading of this volume, to which its merits give it a just claim, must surely result in such increased devotion, as well as in a stronger faith in the God of the promises.

E. J. WOLF.

THEOLOGICAL SEMINARY,
    Gettysburg, Pa.

INTRODUCTION.

To trace the growth of an institution during a number of years, and to give a fair estimate of the real work accomplished, is a task of no small difficulty. The estimate of the real advance made in missionary work in a country whose conditions are so exceptional as those of India, becomes a matter of great perplexity. Small and great are only relative terms. The mission which claims great advance, may have made very little, and the one whose progress has been less marked by the superficial observer, may have made the most substantial progress.

Protestant missions have now been at work a round century, and there have been not wanting those who from the smallness of results would be willing to pronounce them a failure. Taking into account the real advancement made, and the growth of population meanwhile, these would-be philosophers have come to the conclusion that Christian missions can never overtake the rapid and steady growth of Hinduism and Muhammadanism. But we who are engaged in the work do not for a moment forget, that there are other tests than the purely numerical, and that these must not be neglected in a fair estimate of the true growth of Christ's kingdom in India. But just what the progress has been and what stages of development have been reached, no one can exactly determine. Most men want to apply only the test of the numbers that are enlisted in the various missions, without asking themselves the question whether after all such a test is not a very fallacious one in such work and such a land as India.

It is far easier to theorize about the progress of Christian missions than to show actually the state of affairs. This we admit. But while those who are indifferent or hostile have made the slow progress of missions an excuse for their conduct, they have been of use in an indirect way to the friends of missions.

The critic is not so dangerous a man after all as we are sometimes apt to think. In missions, while his efforts are not exactly pleasant, the friends of the great cause, in view of his expected attacks, have been filled with greater carefulness in reporting the progress made to those who have the cause at heart.

Undoubtedly, what all honest men want is to know the facts; and to discover them and faithfully represent them to men in all their bearing on the world-evangelization, is a task, and no light one, which he who would pose as the recorder of the facts in such an important question as the evangelization of the people of India has before him. We may confess, with considerable candor, that, in India, it has been the rule, rather than the exception, in times past, to misrepresent, or rather overestimate, the condition of its people. But such misrepresentation was not intentional. It was only due to the complexity of the subject, and to a too superficial view of all the factors which make up India.

The complex civilization which met the investigator, the unusual social condition which existed, the wide chasm between the different classes of the community, made it difficult to form correct notions of the nation's wealth or poverty, religion, morals, character or life. The same complex organization makes it difficult to represent the progress that Christianity has made.

We have before us a vast field, peopled by a most peculiar people, dominated by most remarkable habits and customs, a people that is not a nation, but rather a combination of different nationalities, each more or less under control of distinct religious and social ideas which differentiate them from each other. This vast population, numbering over 265,000,000, if we include all the dependencies and native states, is under the control of widely different faiths—from the crudest nature-worshipers to the believer in the purest monotheism. All these elements mingle and commingle in the community among which the missionary moves, and render his task one of extreme difficulty.

Socially, morally, and religiously, the situation is most complex. India has its mighty, its rich, its landed proprietors, but there are, too, its poor of every grade to the army of beggars that swarm in its large cities and live in every considerable town. Morally, there have been strange contradictions afloat. He who has lived in the country any length of time is not apt to care to talk much on this subject. The wildest stories are often heard, but it is well to remember that all will depend upon the class of the nation with which you come in contact, and how you have yourself *lived* among the people. It is not an ideal state of morals from any standpoint, but things are neither so good nor so bad as some writers on this subject have been wont to inform the outside world.

Socially, India is a strange land from our western conceptions. Its social conditions are such as to interfere with its progress. This the educated Hindu has been led to see. Reforms many and great are in the air; new marriage laws, proposed for the poor unfortunate widows, left so in childhood, larger liberty to all to embrace and hold what seems reasonable, associations of all sorts in favor of reforms in social matters, are springing up; in short, we shall soon be confronted by a *new social India*.

But religiously there seems to be little change. Here and there new religious associations have been causing a ripple on the surface of the great stagnant pool. That only in a limited sense the native has begun to realize that the centre of all true progress should begin in a true religious life is easily evidenced by the feeble efforts at change in faith. We, of course, do not forget that religious habits and tenets that have, from time out of mind, become rooted in a people's consciousness, are not easily disturbed. And it does not much matter how absurd such views may be from a more enlightened standpoint, that they yield very slowly to the new and untried is only the commonest experience of nations. The very fact of age is regarded by educated and ignorant as a powerful presumptive proof of the vitality of their faith. All these elements make India a difficult field for evangelization. Her elements of weakness are often her elements of strength, especially when the attempt is made to overthrow what has not been clearly seen; for we find men in fighting Hinduism often beating the air, antagonizing what is not really regarded by the people as their faith, and teaching more Hinduism than the majority of their hearers ever knew to exist under that name.

But there is one institution which, while it does not bind but rather separates the different classes from each other, finds those without number who defend it. We mean caste. All agree in their caste views and prejudices. There is little need for our purposes to more than refer to the mastery which caste has over the Hindu people. Caste holds the reign of authority without a rival, and it will not soon let go its hold. The troubles in the infant church are in nine cases out of ten only the recurrence of old-time caste rule, and the great troubles she will have to contend against will be with the same spirit. It takes no prophet to see this. The worst battles of caste will have to be fought out in the Church until this enemy of the true conception of man, this bigot, shall be utterly thrust out and destroyed.

But the spirit of caste makes what is undoubtedly already a hard field ever so much harder. Here is a condition that separates between man and man with terrible persistency, and claims to give great benefit and advantages. But another factor must be referred to in order to get a clear apprehension of the task to which missions have committed themselves.

It is *Brahminism*. Whatever view we may take of the system, it is quite certain that no true view can omit its great power and far-reaching influence. The members of this religious aristocracy are *first* in all matters. They form the strongest barriers to Christianity, for in their community lie entrenched all the powerful endowments of the great temples, as well as all the "arcana" of all that is best in Hinduism. While it is true that in parts of India the followers of the false prophet are many and influential, yet in the main the Brahmin is destined to take the largest part in the affairs and destiny of India and in the history of the Church. He is the natural leader, and the people have acknowledged his leadership for centuries. While Brahmins have not as yet in large numbers embraced the Christian faith, for with Hinduism as now organized the livelihood of the Brahmin is found, yet when once these lower orders of the community embrace the new faith, they will not find it hard to suit their convictions to the changed conditions of their countrymen. The Brahmin must be counted as one of the most formidable enemies that the gospel has to meet. That he will have a large share in the management of the Church in India no one can doubt. Intellectually he has led and present indications show that he will lead the nation. They crowd the government and mission's schools and colleges. They are the most numerously represented on the rolls of universities. The Brahmin has, especially when brought in contact with the truth in mission schools and colleges, the clearest apprehension intellectually of the truths of Christianity, and knows more than any one else how much of western greatness and power are indissolubly bound up with the same. But he holds off because he lacks moral earnestness and the courage of his convictions until he sees certainly whither things are tending. Meanwhile he watches the progress of Christianity, most keenly appreciates its power and perseverance, and is the one who has been most materially benefited by its indirect influences. He occupies a most advantageous position in view of past position and present educational superiority, and this makes him the right hand of British rule in India. While it is true that other classes of the nation are also profiting by the exceptional advantages which have become possible under a wise and benign rule, still they have not, because of racial and social obstacles, availed themselves of these benefits to anything like the extent to which he has.

Brahminism as a system has ever been most mobile, suiting itself in a remarkable degree to the varying circumstances and conditions by and under which it has been surrounded. Its principle has been to absorb by *compromise* all it could in antagonistic systems, and by *supplanting* to win for itself all the ground occupied, claiming to have all the excellencies and none of the evils attached to those systems antagonistic. A very Jacob has it ever been in cunning and shrewdness.

It is this formidable system that must be dealt with by Christianity. Missions and missionaries who make light of the Brahmin, and know him only as the cunning trickster and fulsome, fawning friend, who needs little attention and deserves less, have not fully estimated the chief difficulty which they must meet.

To sum up briefly these elements with which missions have to do you have, (1) A large outcast population, known by different names in different parts of India; aboriginal tribes of many different names, tongues and habits, all lying *outside* the pale of Hinduism, or rather clinging to its skirts, determined to outdo very often their masters in caste-zeal and prejudice; (2) The Muhammadan community, estimated at about 75,000,000 in South India, largely mixed with Hinduism in custom and habit, from which it was most likely largely recruited, somewhat uninfluential in most parts of South India, but influential in the northern parts; (3) The large bulk of the population styled Hindus, of which the Brahmin is the head and the Sudra the foot, including the four ancient castes known as Brahmin, Kshetrya, Vysya and Sudra, but practically divided up into numberless classes. Amid this heterogeneous mass, (for you cannot say their castes are flexible enough to denominate them a nation,) the gospel of Christ is being preached in languages many and dialects strange. In South India alone a dozen or more languages confuse the missionary, and render his progress slow. Add to all this the dense ignorance and superstition of the masses, plunged in a stupid, idolatrous worship for centuries past, and in the hands of cunning priests, who know how to keep and retain power once gained, and you have a field, to say the least, of no special ease, nor does it appeal to such who are anxious to do large things for the Master in a brief lifetime.

This is the field India presents. It is truly not an especially inviting, though certainly a most needy one, to the Christian missionary. But he cannot know the task the Church has set before it for accomplishment until he has actually entered, taken his place in the ranks, and felt the many-sided character which the work presents in this field to be won for Christ—nay, which God has given to His Son for His possession. But the soil has been broken up. Much pioneer work has been done. Christ is no longer an unknown name, especially in the large centres.

A network of missions is being woven, more or less closely, from Ceylon to the Himalayas, and the Church is awakening every day to a clear sense of the great work to be done in this land. Omitting the history of the Roman Catholic missions, which entered India as early as 1542 under Francis Xavier, called the apostle of the Roman church in India, we confine ourselves to a brief review of Protestant missions, so that at a glance one may see what has been done and what is being done to win this land to Christ. It may not be out of place here to note the fact that the Roman church has large and flourishing missions all over the land, and while some may regard them as only little better than heathenism, with a veneer of Christianity, in that they simply substitute to a great extent the adoration of saints and the Virgin for Krishna and heathen deities, we must admit that in large centres of influence they have made great progress. They may be accused, with justice, of tolerating caste, and being not over-careful of the means used to gain their ends, yet they have elements of great power in their sisterhoods and orders of priests, which have contributed not a little to their successes, and which may serve as useful lessons to Protestant missions. As they distribute the Eucharist in only one element, they have little trouble in a land where drinking from a *common cup* is so *defiling!* We cannot but admire the self-sacrifice of many of their missionaries. Would that Protestants could sink everything in the Crucified One as they sink everything in their Church!

Protestant missions began work as early as 1542 in Ceylon, and 1705 in India, on the west coast in Tranquebar. Bartholomew Ziegenbalg and Henry Plustchan, two students of the University of Halle, Germans by nationality and Lutherans in faith, were sent out under the King of Denmark, and to the credit of Halle's pietism, Francke's zeal, and Lutheran training, India owes her first Protestant missionaries, who were on the ground ninety years before any English society, and had done a substantial work when Carey arrived at Calcutta, and owing to the hostility of the English government commenced his great work at Serampore. Ziegenbalg and his companion had made a Tamil translation of the New Testament and a large part of the Old Testament, made many converts, and had begun a most encouraging work, which was carried on by the self-sacrificing labors of the greatest missionary of modern time, often called the apostle of India, Schwartz, with whose death in 1798 we may say the first century of Protestant missions closes.

Slowly the force of missionaries has increased since those early days until all countries have joined in the work of India's evangelization and missionaries have penetrated into all parts of the land.

The latest statistics give 74 organizations with 975 foreign missionaries, ordained and unordained, divided between Great Britain, the Continent and the United States, with quite a number from other lands.

This is the foreign force. To this must be added an ordained native agency of 797 and an unordained of 3,491 (1890). From the beginning of the work up to 1886, there were 2,423 foreign missionaries, clerical and others, and 28,568 native ordained and others. The Danish society ceased to exist or rather was merged into others, while of many others the same may be said, though no influence has been lost and thousands have blessed the day that saw the foreign missionaries enter this caste-ridden, idolatrous land. All the forces at work now are organized as never before, and though some differences on minor modes of work may exist, there is yet a most substantial agreement among all missionaries as to the central ideas that must mark mission aggression, and as to the chief means to be used in the warfare against entrenched and deeply-rooted existing systems of belief. We occupy the vantage ground of an army that by experience has learned its foe's power, resources and strength. Of the general work accomplished it is not the purpose of this sketch to speak, but we have a much humbler task to perform. Among the American missions that have held an honored place in India's evangelization stands the one which is to form the subject of *this Historical Sketch: the American Evangelical Lutheran, founded in 1842, and working among the Telugus in the Krishna District of the Madras Presidency*, on the south side of the Krishna River, one of the twelve sacred rivers of the Hindus.

AFTER FIFTY YEARS.

CHAPTER I.

THE FOUNDING OF THE MISSIONARY SOCIETY IN AMERICA.

It was only natural that a Church whose founders had sat at the feet of Francke and drank in his spirit and the spirit of pietists of Halle should be early awakened to their duty of preaching the gospel to the Gentiles.

The Lutheran Church of America was largely German, with Danish, Swedish, Norwegian, Dutch, and other elements. Its early struggle to establish itself in the United States of America forms one of the most interesting chapters of American Church History. About the same time that Xavier was reaping his first fruits in India, the Lutheran Church was gaining a permanent foothold in the western world; in 1638 the Swedes, on the banks of the Delaware river, established the first organization of Lutherans on the American continent. From this date rapid progress was made, though in the face of bitter opposition and persecution. For several centuries the internal condition of the Church was such as to leave little or no room to consider the needs of the lands in darkness. The Church was largely dependent on foreign pastors; was, in fact, a foreign mission field from the standpoint of the Fatherland Church, which also performed out-and-out foreign work among the aboriginal tribes. Thus for a hundred and more years internal needs were so great that the work of the more needy nations could not be taken up, or the internal struggles for life were so intense that self-existence was about as much as could be maintained.

But the devout spirit of Muhlenberg and his helpers never for a moment forgot the "great commission" of the Lord, and as soon as the Church was fairly on its feet the question of Foreign Missions and the heathen world came up for a hearing and solution in a practical form. No one seems to have met the call to labor as it was elsewhere met, with the astonishing announcement that when God wanted to convert the heathen He would do so.

Without human suggestion or help, the first general body of the Church met in convention in 1820, and at its meeting the spirit of missions expressed itself in the determination "to form a missionary institute." The first English journal (1826) contains an article on Foreign Missions. That this work was not undertaken earlier must not be put down to a want of willingness or sympathy, but to the great needs of the work at home, which was far beyond the Church's ability to supply with an adequate ministry or the stated means of grace, owing to the lack of qualified men in a new country, where education was in its infancy, and to the vast district over which the members of the Church were scattered, as well as to the rapid growth from foreign emigration.

However, the General Synod of 1833, held in the city of Baltimore, urged the subject of missions upon the District Synods, and determined to hold a missionary meeting at the next sitting of that body. It should be noted, however, that previous to this time, although no Lutheran missionary from the American Church was in the field, funds had been contributed in considerable amounts through the American Board, at that early date about the only society regularly organized in America for carrying the blessed gospel to the nations in darkness. In 1835 a most earnest report was presented, in which the arguments on behalf of Foreign Missions were eloquently set forth, urging upon all ministers the necessity of preaching on the subject to their people, and concluding the report by advocating that "as soon as possible" their efforts should be extended to the conversion of the heathen. The General Synod accepted this report, and recommended the holding of a missionary convention at the meeting of the West Pennsylvania Synod in October the same year, and urged the District Synods to establish a Foreign Mission.

As a fruit of this convention the "Central Missionary Society" was formed, which, in the words of its constitution, was "to send the gospel of the Son of God to the destitute parts of the Southern Church * * * to assist such congregations for a season * * * as were unable to support themselves, and *ultimately to co-operate in* sending it (the gospel) to the heathen."

Its first care was what we now style Home Missions, but the deep need of Foreign Missions, and the Church's responsibility thereto, were not for a moment forgotten.

While these things were transpiring at home, letters were received from Lutheran missionaries in China and India, Gutzlaff and Rheinus (died 1838) appealing for help in their respective fields. This was regarded as the clearest indication that God was ordering the Church, through the call of these faithful servants, to begin the work of Foreign Missions, and all agreed "that Rheinus must be sustained." It should be added that he and some of his associates, members of the Lutheran Church, and laboring under the Church Missionary Society, had withdrawn on the ground that they could not accept the Episcopacy as it was taught in the Church of England. Sherring justly remarks, in regard to this matter, that it is quite possible that both parties were right, by which, of course, he means that on this question there is room for difference of opinion; but there could be no room for two systems of church government to grow on the same mission foundation. Endless trouble could only result if Rheinus and his colleagues had been given their way, and Rheinus and his associates would have been untrue to their teaching and Church if they had admitted the claims of Episcopal ordination over their own. Almost one-fourth of the entire membership followed Rheinus and his party, and for a time it looked as if a permanent breach had been made. It was to assist this work that Rheinus made his plea before the American churches.

In 1837 the General Synod's committee on the subject of Foreign Missions in its report expressed the conviction that as our District Synods were ready for the work, the General Synod should express its opinion on the question, and urged that an organization should be effected by holding a convention, that the call of Rheinus and Gutzlaff be deemed providential, that all *German* churches be asked to coöperate irrespective of ecclesiastical connection, and that the plan adopted should in its opinion embrace in it a *connection with the American Board.*

The convention urged met early in 1837, and organized the society known as the German Foreign Missionary Society, "the intention being to enlist the sympathy of all individuals of 'German descent' or association in the United States." It was also resolved to assist Rheinus as soon as satisfactory answers could be received from him and his colleagues as to the cause of their separation from the Church Missionary Society. Suffice it to say letters were received and funds were subsequently sent, and from individuals and District Synods additional help was forwarded, the Synod of South Carolina alone appropriating $500 for a *printing press* for the Mission.

While these things were pending, the General Synod

met 1837), and the zeal in the Foreign Mission cause being still on the increase, Rev. Wm. Heilig and others offered themselves as missionaries if the Church was willing to send them. But as no answer had been received from the German Reformed Churches, and on subsequent correspondence it being found that they were not prepared to unite with the Lutheran Churches in this work, at the next meeting of the Missionary Society its name was changed to that of the "Foreign Missionary Society of the Evangelical Lutheran Church in the United States."

Rheinus died in 1838, and the rest of the seceders returned to the Church Missionary Society, so that no special call came for funds from that quarter, and the Society felt free to start independent work. In the spring of 1840, the Rev. C. F. Heyer, of Carlisle, Pa., offered himself and received the appointment as missionary of the new Society, and began to prepare for his departure to India. Unfortunately misunderstandings arose as to the relation of the missionary to the American Board, which had been consulted as to the operations of the new Mission, and through which it was proposed to transact its business, and although it was distinctly understood that the Mission was to be independent, the plan of union adopted was strongly opposed, and while no hostility was shown to the American Board, it was deemed best by many that our operations should be in no way subject to another body. The union with the American Board was dropped, though not before the Rev. Heyer, fearing it might be consummated, had resigned his appointment. The mother Synod, the Synod of Pennsylvania, had all along preserved a more or less independent attitude toward the General Synod (for quite a number of years, 1823 to 1853, not participating in the meeting of the latter body), keeping up an independent missionary organization. At this time it was only natural for the missionary who had resigned his appointment, as noted above, to turn to this Missionary Society and offer his services to them. He was appointed forthwith, and made preparations to leave for India in October, 1841.

We have gone thus minutely into the matter to show the Rev. Heyer's standing toward the General Synod, and the reason he did not come to India as a representative of that body, and especially because it seems to us that the Rev. Mr. Trabert, in his brief sketch, entitled "Missions among the Telugus," has not gone into the history of the missionary movement with sufficient fulness to relieve it from misunderstanding. He fails to show the history of Father Heyer's relation to the General Synod's Society, and ignores the active spirit of Missions which prevailed in all parts of the Lutheran Church at that time. Certainly the facts show it was no lack either of missionary zeal or organization in those synods which then coöperated in the General Synod that prevented Father Heyer from going to India as the missionary of that Body, but simply a fear on his part, and one shared by many others, as subsequent events showed, that he might not find coöperation with the American Board and its missionaries conducive to the best interests of the work. As Lutheran workers, as in the case of Rheinus, had come in conflict with the Church of England missionaries, it was best to form any further unions with extreme caution. He and others doubtless feared, and not without good reason, that the development along the lines of Christian work in their Church would not be best subserved by union with other bodies, however full of evangelical zeal and piety they might be, and we cannot blame them. However, let us add, that missionary zeal was in no way confined to any part of our Church in America; all parts alike felt the spirit of missions to be the spirit of true Christianity. Though the General Synod did not unite in sending Father Heyer to India the first time, the spirit of missions was never stronger in that body than when he left for his foreign field in 1841, as is abundantly shown by the fact that in 1843 it commissioned and sent out the Rev. Walter Gunn, and instructed him, if expedient, to coöperate with the missionary of the Pennsylvania Synod. Thus while the credit of sending the first missionary is due to the mother Synod of the Lutheran Church in America, the spirit of the children in the General Synod was no whit behind in zeal or interest.

Suffice it to say the Rev. Gunn was most warmly welcomed by Father Heyer, and when, in 1846, he returned to America on account of ill health, the whole burden of the work devolved on brother Gunn, whereupon the old Synod expressed her entire willingness to transfer the whole management to the General Synod's Society, while continuing to support the Mission with her contributions. It would therefore be a mistake to take away any glory due to the mother Synod, but it would equally be so to represent, or fail to represent, the facts in such way as to create the impression that the zeal of any part of the Church was prior to that of other parts. Dr. Wolf, in his "Lutherans in America," has clearly pointed out the value of the early organization of the General Synod. He declares that it "sounded the keynote" in beneficent movements in the Church. "For half a century it was the most conspicuous and influential factor in advancing the usefulness and glory" of the Church.

We have attempted to sketch as clearly and fully as space and the purpose of this book would allow, the early beginning of our Foreign Mission work in America. We have not spoken of its present organization, though much more could be said. We must turn our attention now to a consideration of the field to which the missionary came, and in which he has labored with varying success for more than half a century.

CHAPTER II.

THE GENERAL SYNOD'S MISSION FIELD.

THE Madras Presidency comprises that part of India, which lies between the 8th degree northern latitude and the 20th, and the 74th degree east longitude and the 85th. Its greatest length is 950 miles, and its greatest breadth 475, with an area of about 141,000 square miles. It is three times the size of the State of New York. Lying along the sea-coast mainly, and within the torrid zone, with no mountains over 8000 feet in altitude, subject to extreme seasons of drought, with a mean temperature of about 80°, the climate is extremely hot for nine months in the year. Rains in various portions differ very much in frequency. Along the coast, there may be an average rain-fall of 70 inches, while in the upland districts, it will barely reach 10 inches per annum. The Presidency is divided for governmental purposes into twenty-two districts. In these there is a population of 39,331,062 (1891).

There are spoken Tamil, Telugu, Malayalam, Kanarese, Uriya and Hindustani, besides other dialects. We are concerned in this sketch with only one, the Telugu, which is spoken by 13,653,674 within the Presidency and by about 6,000,000 in other parts, in the Nizam's dominions, Mysore and elsewhere. Telugu or Tenugu, as otherwise pronounced, is one of the Dravidian languages, and for form and beauty, holds the first place. Many of the words are from the classical Sanscrit, specially all scientific, theological and polite forms. The Telugus, as well as their tongue, are allied to the old Scythian stock, and only a long connection with

SACRED BULL IDOL.

the old Aryan race, a union of a superior with an inferior race, socially and intellectually, has almost given a Sanscrit form to their literature and language. The Aryan portion of the population now speak the Telugu, which they have largely changed, and on account of the lapse of time, few if any continue to speak in the old Sanscrit. Whether Aryan or Telugu, all have come to speak the language of the conquered, Telugu, though with much modification and great improvement in form and wealth of expression.

Of the twenty-two districts into which the Presidency is divided, those in which the Telugus mainly dwell, lie north of the city of Madras, the metropolis of south

A GROUP OF SERVANTS.

India, a city of 452,518 population, and bear the following names: Ganjam, Vizagapatam, Godavery, Krishna, Bellary, Cuddapah, Kurnool, Nellore (parts only) and North Arcot districts. In the city of Madras, as well as in other large cities in India, the Telugu is spoken by large numbers.

We shall trace briefly the work of Missions among these Telugu peoples, during the times immediately preceding the occupancy of the field by our Mission.

Our Mission founder, 'Father' Heyer, arrived in the Krishna district early in 1842. The writer of "Missions among the Telugus," seems to think that he in-intended to work with Rheinus, but such cannot have been his intention, as that worthy missionary had died in 1838, and his colleagues had shortly after returned to the Church Mission Society from which they had withdrawn. The condition of the Telugu country as a mission field, on the advent of Father Heyer to India, is worth noting. As yet little had been done for these people.

It is true the Roman Catholic Missions were on the ground, and had already fairly entrenched themselves at different points. From all accounts, the French Jesuits were the first to enter the Telugu country, and founded the Carnatic Mission, which penetrated into the heart of Telugu districts. But though they have never made a strong fight against existing caste customs, and have, in fact, more or less encouraged, by their Church customs, the old ideas, they have advanced slowly. As they give the holy communion only in *one element*, it would be supposed that their advantage would be great in reaching those whose customs make a *common cup* most distasteful to them. But such does not seem to have been the result. Their efforts have been also largely confined to the better classes, those within the pale of the Hindu community; and though so much earlier on the ground than Protestants, their progress has been very slow.

Protestant Missions began considerably later, and reached out into the Telugu country little earlier than 1800 A. D., and then only very feebly at first. The first organization was that of the London Missionary Society at Vizagapatam in 1805, but no converts were gained before 1835, a period of 30 years, though much hard work had been done, and the Bible translated, at least in part, into the vernacular tongue of the people.

HEATHEN TEMPLE ON A FEAST DAY.

In 1818, Revs. Gordon and Pritchett published the whole New Testament, which was the only copy of the New Testament available for more than 30 years. The Old Testament was roughly translated about the same time, but was not, it seems, printed until 1850, when the Revs. Johnson and Gordon (son of the missionary above mentioned), prepared final proofs for the press for the Madras Auxiliary Bible Society. It seems that God raised up this Mission at Vizagapatam for the special work of translation. It has always led the way, and the last days of one of South India's greatest missionaries were spent in a careful revision of existing editions of the Telugu scriptures. Dr. John Hay was most wonderfully fitted for this work both by his residence of almost fifty years and by his ripe scholarship. But, with the exception of this invaluable work of biblical translation, little had been accomplished toward the conversion of the heathen. The native church had only *fourteen* members (communicants) in 1841. Yet these servants of God were accomplishing a work, the results of which cannot be estimated.

Following the establishment of this Mission in point of time, was that of the same English society in Bellary, Cuddapah and Kurnool districts, the two latter of which are inhabited almost entirely by Telugus. Work was commenced in 1810. But here, as elsewhere, it was maintained by a small staff of European workers for more than thirty years, the Rev. Hands receiving reinforcements not earlier than 1840, when the Rev. Dawson joined him. It may be doubted whether much thorough work could be undertaken by two or three men, who were called upon to administer the varied interests of so vast a field, but a small congregation of native Christians was gathered into the Church as early as 1844.

The next Society to enter the Telugu country was the American Baptist, which was brought about by the English Baptist Mission of Orissa. The Rev. S. S. Day was the pioneer of this work, and arrived in 1836. He, however, took up no permanent station, but remained for some time at Vizagapatam and Chicacole in the extreme north of the Telugu country, in 1837, removing to Madras. Here he did some English work among the soldiers, and organized a Baptist Church for Englishmen and Eurasians* in 1838. Not till 1840 did he fix upon a permanent mission station with Nellore as its centre. In 1844, though he had traveled far and wide, to Guntur and Hyderabad, his church numbered only eight members. From this time, the Mission struggled for life. In 1848 the home committee determined to close the Mission; it was then that it got the sobriquet of the "Lone Star." Again in 1862, for want of success, it was about to be closed, and was only continued at the earnest request of the sainted Dr. Jewett, who devoted his whole life to the field. It has, of recent years, had what is generally regarded phenomenal success by the churches at home, but which must be estimated, as must all results in such a land as India, with considerable caution from a true missionary standpoint. Without any desire to criticise or to disparage the great work done, it is to be feared that *numbers* have been too

---

* Of mixed European and native parentage. A large and influential class in parts of India, though often very poor and miserable, with neither European energy nor native simplicity.

much glorified. Its success has been largely among the outcastes of the nation, among whom other missions have been reaping large harvests.

Following close on the heels of the Baptists of America, we find the Godavery Delta Mission, under the control of no denomination, which began its work at Masulipatam in 1836, but removed, the same year, to Narsapur, about 40 miles from the former place, in the delta of the Godavery river. For six years they saw no fruit of their labors, but at length, a poor shoemaker accepted the way of life, and others followed, until in 1842 there was a Christian community of 30 souls.

The Church Mission Society began its Mission in the Krishna district at Masulipatam, through Revs. Noble and Fox, the first representatives, who arrived in 1841, September 28th, and who laid the foundation of a solid and a remarkable mission work, on the firm basis of the gospel, with a due regard for all classes and parts of the Hindu community. Since then they have carried on a successful and ever-increasing work. The progress has been steady rather than phenomenal. They have labored with great fidelity for fifty years, and have been richly blessed in their work. They number many of all classes in their churches. With a work well organized, they are now reaping large accessions from the humbler classes, though under the sainted Noble, 25 converts, mostly from the Brahmin class, were won. His self-denying labors live in the lives of many.

A number of other Missions have since then sprung

up in different parts of the Telugu country, the most flourishing of these being: the Hermansburg Lutheran Mission, commenced in 1866 by Rev. Mylius, who came out at the earnest request of Rev. C. Grönning, and for a while remained at Rajahmundry, expecting to work there; the Society for Propagation of the Gospel in the Kurnool and Cuddapah districts; and the Canadian Baptist, organized at Cacanada in 1875.

From the foregoing sketch, it can be easily seen, that, when Rev. C. F. Heyer entered the Telugu country, little had been done and ample room was found for his work. Only a few struggling communities were to be found in all the vast region among the millions therein, and the great multitude had as yet been untouched by missionary influence. The founder of the Lutheran Missions of the Krishna district, sent out by the Synod of Pennsylvania, arrived in India early in 1842. Proceeding from Columbo, via Palamcottah, Tanjore, Tranquebar, he visited the flourishing Missions at these places on his way, and under the advice of missionary friends, he was directed to the Telugu country, as a field little occupied. He reached Guntur, 250 miles north of Madras, on the 31st of July, 1842. On every side he turned, he was confronted with heathenism of the most determined kind. No missionary was nearer to him than Masulipatam, 50 miles away. The American Baptist missionary was at Nellore, 140 miles away, the London still further, the North German missionary more than 100 miles, at Rajahmundry, and the country to be evangelized by him densely peopled by those sunken in the deepest ignorance of their true nature, and of God, and of their relation to Him. It would have appalled a less resolute soul to have begun work under such circumstances!

FOUR GENERATIONS.

The immediate field, however, taken up by him, was that part of the Krishna district lying on the south bank of the Krishna river, one of the twelve sacred rivers of the Hindus, and bounded on the south by the Nellore district. The whole district is divided into eleven subdivisions, called taluks, seven of which lie on the south side of the Krishna river, viz., Palnad, Satenapalli, Narasarowpet, Vinakonda, Guntur, Bapatla and Repalli, and form what has always been regarded the field of the General Synod's Mission. For our pur-

A MUHAMMADAN WOMAN.

pose, it is unnecessary to speak at present of the northern part of the Krishna district, occupied by the Church Missionary Society since 1841.

But a more minute reference to these seven divisions will be in place. In general among the twenty-two districts the Krishna district ranks fourth in size, eleventh in population, and second in point of revenue from all sources, in the Madras Presidency. Its population, according to the census of 1881, was 1,548,480, of whom there were as follows:

Hindus proper *	1,425,013
Muhammadans	87,161
Christians, Roman Catholic and Protestant	36,194
Jains, Buddhist and others	112

The growth of population may be seen by comparing the census of 1881 and 1891, which shows an interesting fact concerning the increase of the Christian population which is encouraging.

	1881.	1891.	Rate of increase.
Hindus	1,425,013	1,678,333	17%
Muhammadans	87,161	108,567	24%
Christians	36,194	68,524	89%
Jains, Buddhists and others	112	145	
The total population	1,548,480	1,855,582	19%

* Hindus comprise 17 castes or subdivisions; of these, the outcastes, according to Hindu custom, from whom most Christians come, form 20 per cent. of the whole population.

The wealth of the district lies largely in its extensive cotton and indigo cultivation in the upland Taluks, and in its vast rice fields in the lowlands, irrigated by the Krishna river. The Department of Public Works projected a scheme of irrigation which has developed the resources of the district to a wonderful extent. It is by means of this that famine is warded off. There are 384 miles of canal open to navigation. These canals are fed by a large dam thrown across the Krishna river at Bezwada, the length of which is about three-quarters of a mile, its height twenty feet above the deep bed of the stream, and its width at top six feet, and the whole structure backed by 400,000 cubic yards of rough stone, sloping away firm from the wall 257 feet down stream. This immense dam supplies water sufficient to irrigate 470,000 acres, and cost the government 16,670,-813 rupees; as a mere financial undertaking it has annually netted 941,132 rupees, or over six per cent. on the outlay. But when the untold misery of a famine is remembered, and what a powerful protection it furnishes against it, then surely no one can begin to compute the benefit it has been to this district, and directly or indirectly to all India.

On the uplands, grain or as government would say dry-crops of all kinds are raised. The most valuable of these products are the cotton and indigo, for which an extensive demand exists in Europe. As seen below,*

---

* Table at close of this chapter.

36 per cent. of the population are classed under farmers, so that a large proportion of the people live on the products of the soil. Very little has been done to develop the mineral resources of the country, though undoubtedly India is rich in minerals. It will take western enterprise to open these. Already gold, coal and other minerals, not to mention diamonds, have drawn western capital.

The natural features of the Krishna district are rather uninteresting. A chain of low hills, spurs of the eastern Ghats, traverses its whole extent, rising to the height of 1700 feet above sea level, and 1520 feet above the plain, bearing on the south side of the Krishna river the name Kondavida, and on the north, Kondapalli. Both hills bear evidence of having been formerly strongly fortified. The former was taken and retaken during the stormy Muhammadan period. The French took it in 1757. It is rich in remains that would repay the labors of the archæologist. The land lying along the foot of these, between them and the Bay of Bengal, is a level plain, rising little above sea level. To the west of these hills, the country is more broken and rugged, while the Palnad Taluk is surrounded by hills, and decidedly rolling.

The geological formation is of considerable interest. As far as thirty miles inland, remains of the ocean, shells and other sea products, are found. The whole coast was evidently reclaimed from the sea in early times. There is, however, a great mixture of black cotton, red shale and limestone conglomerate to be found all along the coast. The foot hills are thrusts, and have been due to igneous action, while the Palnad hills are shale, and have resulted from pressure and have not come under powerful igneous agency. The rock in these formations grades from a granite, hard and unstratified, to a metamorphic rock. The granitoid furnishes an excellent building stone, and can easily be burned loose and broken in perfect layers, ready for the mason's hammer and chisel.

The government of this part of India, at present, furnishes no special feature for consideration. It was under the rule of various powers in the past. Hindu Rajas held sway for many centuries, until the Muhammadan invasion of India in the thirteenth century.

The Emperor of Delhi had at least nominal control for about four hundred years. Then followed a period of French ascendency in south India under M. de Bussi and M. Duplex. However, during this period the English merchants of the East India Company were laying the foundation of English empire in this as well as in other parts of India. In May, 1759, the treaty was signed by which the districts of Masulipatam and Nizampatam were handed over to the English. The country, however, around Guntur, and westward, remained under other rule for many years; even thirteen years after the relinquishment of it to the English by the Emperor of Delhi, it was still under the Nizam of Hyderabad, and did not pass under the control of the company till *September, 1788*. The whole country has since been brought under one central control, and is now known as the Krishna district, with its seat of government at Masulipatam.

The revenue department is under a collector, assisted by two subdivisional European and one native deputy collectors, who have their offices at Guntur, Bezwada and Vinakonda. The officers are assisted by a large staff of clerks, and besides having all revenue matters under their control, are also vested with magisterial powers. The Taluks, of which we shall speak more particularly by and by, have each a native official called a Tahsildar, who is the right hand man of the European official, and who until recently had also magisterial powers conferred on him. Under these officials, there are inspectors of revenue, and these in turn examine into the condition of the crops, and gather all information from the petty village officers, the Kurnam and Munsiff. The people in our part of India live in villages, and the old village system of the ancient times, with but slight modifications, has come down to us. The village officials hold their offices on life tenure, or during good behavior, and transmit them to their offspring. The centre of all this official life is the collector, who really seems a little monarch in his district, especially so to one accustomed to republican simplicity. India's government is central to a fault; it is a perfect bureaucracy.

The judicial work is carried on partly by the revenue

officers, as above noted, and partly by a European judge, resident at Masulipatam, assisted by a staff of native officials, who preside over courts, termed Munsiff courts, with powers to try all civil cases under 2000 Rs. The sessions court is the final resort of all who are dissatisfied with the decisions of the lower courts, and is the final judge in all cases under 7000 Rs. The Hindu has been repeatedly described as very litigious, and there seems to be ground for the charge, when you hear judicial officers speaking of the long files of undisposed suits, and hundreds yet waiting for their turn on the files. The Munsiffs have nothing to do with criminal suits, but the sessions judge must take up all sorts of cases, though his heaviest work is that of appeals from the decisions of the lower courts.

Along with the judicial department, we must also mention the police. They are organized under a European superintendent and his assistant, with a large subordinate staff of inspectors and European head constables. The native police is armed, and under regular military drill; it furnishes the arm not only for the suppression and detection of all manner of crime, but is also expected to keep down riots and disturbances of a social or national character, which, at any time, may arise between the different religious communities.

The department that has done great things for the country, let men say what they may, is the Department of Public Works. We have already noticed the large irrigation work under its control. They are able to carry out other schemes—extension of tanks, and large plans of irrigation; and they are undoubtedly the most useful arm of the government, and add millions every year to the public revenue.

The departments of salt and abkari (spirits) and of forest should also be noticed. The former has been made to bear no small share of blame within the last few years, salt being made a government monopoly, and spirits being made a source of revenue. This systematic supply of spirits by the government, it has been contended, has increased the consumption of native spirits, although the defense of the government is that the supply is only brought under proper regulations and limited by well-framed rules.

The educational department, through which the government is trying to enlighten India's masses, cannot be forgotten in this hasty review, inasmuch as Missions have ever gotten the greatest encouragement through this arm of the government service, by means of liberal grants-in-aid toward the maintenance of their schools and colleges. The present policy of this department is to foster and encourage vernacular and primary schools, and let higher and college education take care of itself, assisting it only by means of a grant from public funds. This is in accordance with the famous educational despatch of 1854, and is a wise policy. But it will be necessary to refer to this subject later on, as we turn now to a brief survey of the Taluks or township in which the Mission has labored.

We begin with the extreme western part of the Krishna district,

PALNAD TALUK,

which is more or less shut off from the rest of the district, being separated from the Vinakonda and Sattinapalli Taluks by high hills, and from the Nizam dominion by the Krishna river. Palnad means the country

GROUP OF ELEPHANTS.

of hamlets, and has an area of 1000 square miles. Toward the close of the sixteenth century, this portion of the Krishna district came into historical notice, when it was an asylum for defeated chieftains from other parts of southern India. When the great Mogul empire was divided, the Palnad fell to the Navab of Arcot, who exacted from the chiefs of the Taluk, for over thirty years, large annual revenues. It was occupied by English troops about 1766. Such were the exactions upon the poor people by the chief officers of the Navab, "that the people, oppressed beyond power of sufferance, fled from villages and fields." In 1787 it was mortgaged by the Navab to the East India Company, and in 1790 was first brought under English rule. But for a number of years thereafter, though the chieftains were pensioned to keep them quiet, the country was greatly disturbed, and "a lamentable state of affairs, with no security of life or property," existed. In 1801 it was ceded to the Company, and after some of the marauding bands were dispersed, and their chiefs killed, the country had rest. The chief town of the Taluk is Dachepalli. The Roman Catholics have a Mission at Rentachintala. Other places of importance are Turmakorta, Karempudi and Veldurti. The country is hilly and is less densely settled than other parts of the district; the soil less fertile. The great military road from Madras to Hyderabad passes through the Taluk, and there are excellent roads connecting it with Guntur, through Narasarowpet and Satenapalli. Directly south of this Taluk lies

VINUKONDA TALUK.

Vinukonda, the chief town, lies at the foot of a hill, which gives name to both town and Taluk. Vinukonda means the "Hill of Hearing," and is, in legend, supposed to be the place where Rama heard the news of his wife Seta's misfortunes. Another derivation of the word is "little hill." The hill, cleft by volcanic or other action, was the seat of an ancient Hindu temple. The English got possession of the fortifications and the Taluk, at the close of the eighteenth century, demolish-

SCENE IN VINUKONDA.

ing the former. The Pindaris, a wild banditti tribe, laid waste the Taluk as late as 1816, robbing and killing the people in great numbers. By a geological survey, the Taluk shows unmistakable signs of early occupation, and at different places stone circles, similar to the Druid, remain. To the patient research of the archæologist, the Taluk presents a rich field. The wild jungle tribes inhabit this and the Palnad Taluk. They are known under the name *Chensu*, are rude in dress (or rather dressless) and manners, and worship their bows and arrows or other weapons of war or chase. They speak a rude Telugu. The Taluk is accessible by good roads, and is traversed by the Southern Maratta Railway. Passing east from Vinukonda, we enter the

NARASAROWPET TALUK.

Its soil and general aspect of the country is very similar to that of Vinukonda. Near the principal town, Narasarowpet, whose name is derived from a former Zemindar, rises boldly out of the plains a hill called *Kolappa Konda*, while on the eastern side, separating it from Guntur Taluk, stretch the Kondavedu hills, to which allusion has already been made. These latter hills form the theatre of many stories and legends. They were strongly fortified in former times, and the French thought the hills too steep to scale, and regarded them as impregnable, unless the garrison was starved. One of the legends may be narrated, which will give a fair idea of much of the early history of this land.

A cowherd used to drive his cows to the hill, near an image of Venkatamma, where lived a hermit who did penance, and to whom the former gave milk. By and by, the hermit told the cowherd to dig under a certain bush and he would be rewarded. After digging several days and finding nothing, he ceased, when the hermit, who was looking on, ordered him to throw the bush

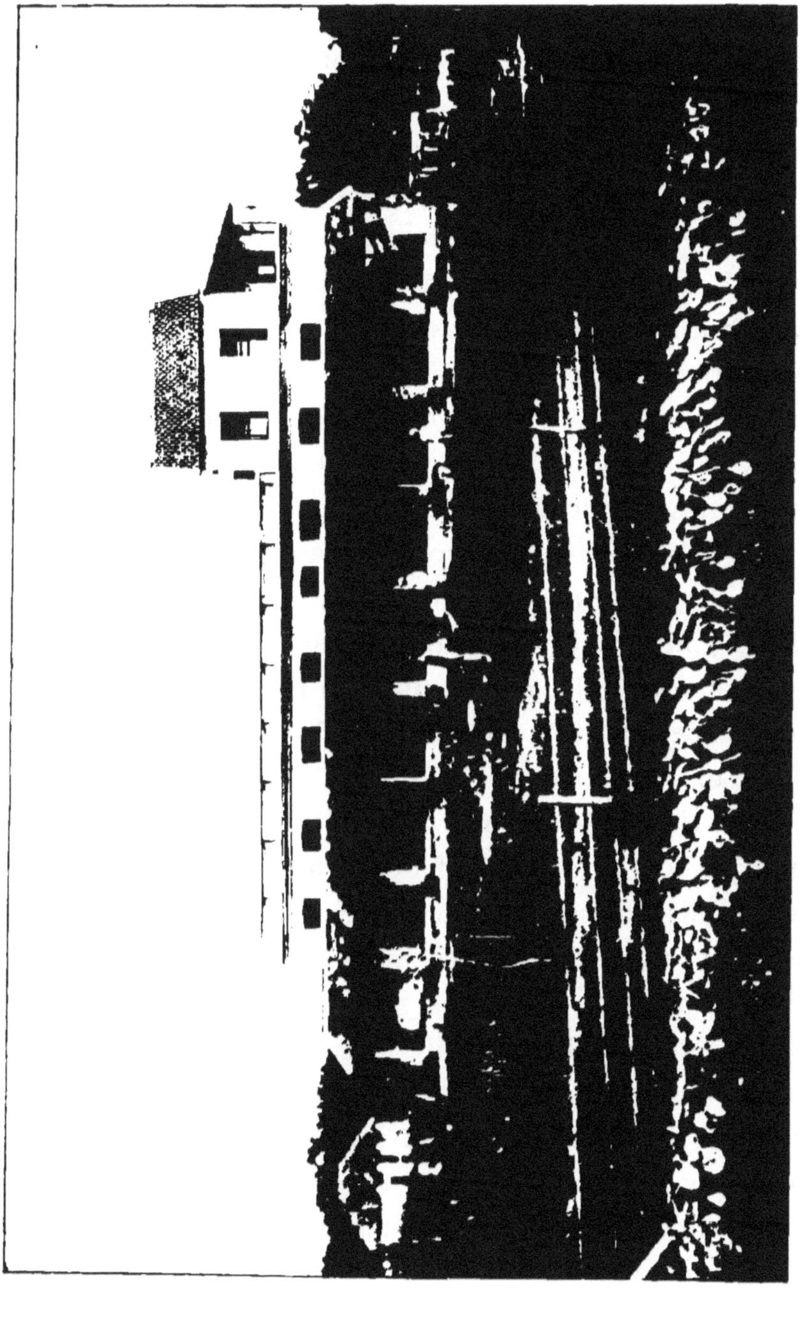

NICHOLS MEMORIAL BUNGALOW, NARASAROWPET.

into the hole he was digging and set it on fire. While watching it burning he was forcibly seized by the hermit, who tried to throw him into the flames. At once he apprehended the situation—the deity must have a *human sacrifice* in order to give up her treasure—so being the stronger man, he pushed the hermit in and fled. Returning next day and looking into the pit, sure enough his supposition was found correct; the sacrifice had appeased the evil spirit, and among the ashes he discovered an image of gold. He secretly carried it home, and ignorant of its worth, he exchanged bits of it from time to time at a shop for betel-nut and other luxuries. The shop-keeper growing very rich, the story of his wealth came to the king's ears, and enquiries being made by him as to the source of his wealth, the whole story came to light, and resulted in the banishing of the shop-keeper and the confiscation of the image.

But to return to the history, the Taluk was made over to the English in 1788. The old palace of the kings stands in a state of decay at Narasarowpet, all their lands having been taken under English control, and the present Zemindar being a pensioner of the English government.

The Kotappa Konda hill is famous as the seat of a temple, and the place of an annual pilgrimage. Thousands of people from all parts of the country visit the shrine on the hill, and attend the fair, at which all sorts of trading in Hindu commodities are carried on in connection with the annual religious festival. The temple is of modern construction, 1750 A. D. being its probable date. It is approached by a winding flight of steps, and is situated about 600 feet above the level of the plain, the hill itself being 1587 feet above sea level. The festival is a regular fair, to which traders come from all parts. Lying to the north of it is the

SATENAPALLI TALUK,

bounded by the Krishna river on the north, the Palnad Taluk on the west, and Guntur Taluk on the east. Until recently, Krossur was the seat of the Taluk government, but lately it has been moved to Satenapalli, a town twenty-one miles west of Guntur. Bellamkonda was formerly a strongly fortified hill, and played a very important part in the Hindu and Muhammadan wars.

The most interesting place in the Taluk, and perhaps in all this part of India, from an archæological standpoint, is Amaravati, and its adjoining town, Dharanikota, situated on the banks of the Krishna. Hindus say that the temple here is 4000 years old, but as they are scarcely ever correct in any of their dates, it might be well to reduce its antiquity by a few thousand years! Coins have been found in the towns that date back, however, to the first century A. D. Here were discovered the famous Buddhist remains and carvings, which were first brought to light by the native king, while hunting for materials to build his palace. Some of them are to be seen in the British museum. Their age must be before A. D., and in Dr. Burgess' opinion, the ruins discovered were covered by a flood and so preserved. To the east lies the

GUNTUR TALUK,

which is an open plain skirted by the Kondavedu hills on the west. The soil is red shale, with a considerable stretch of black cotton in the southern part of the

SUB-COLLECTOR'S BUNGALOW, GUNTUR.

Taluk. So level in fact is it that the Krishna has backed up its waters within a few miles of Guntur at high flood. Guntur is the natural centre of the district, and should be the centre of its government. At present the sub-collector resides here, but prior to 1877 the head officials, both revenue and judicial, resided here.

The town has its own municipal government, largely

in the control of native gentlemen, and presided over by a native chairman. A telegraph office, civil dispensary, police station, sub-collector's offices, Munsiff's court, constitute the chief government buildings. The name probably signifies *tank*, and was an insignificant village in 1679. After passing through the hands of the Muhammadans and French, it was at length ceded to

HINDU TEMPLE IN GUNTUR.

the English in 1788. The town is the centre of a considerable cotton trade, there being three steam presses and a large ginning factory located here. Before 1860, it was considered a very unhealthy place; but since then, through the efforts of European officials, and stricter sanitary regulations, the place is regarded as a fairly healthy one, though at times it seems in danger of getting back its bad name. The Southern Maratta Railway passes near the town, and the Madras Bezwada Railway has been projected with a branch line to Guntur. A new town is being laid out near the railway station, called Arundelpet, after a former very energetic collector. The population has increased over 4000 during the last decade. During April and May the heat is excessive, though 30 miles away, along the Bay of Bengal, it is more bearable. The district jail formerly located here has been abolished. There is a small congregation of the Church of England here.

Guntur is the center of our Mission work. Here are located our college (the Watts Memorial), boys and girls boarding schools, Zenana work and new hospital and dispensary, besides four residences of missionaries and a neat brick church, the Stork memorial, and all the necessary buildings for the prosecution of the varied work of the Mission.

The Roman Catholics have tried to maintain a mission here, but with very indifferent success; their strong missions being at Firangipuram and Patabandla, in Satenapalli Taluk, and at Muthuru in this Taluk. Guntur being the centre of the cotton trade for these parts, large quantities are pressed and shipped to Europe by local agents. Five main roads meet in the town, the great northern road being the most important, and a highway from Madras, 250 miles to the south, to Calcutta, over 800 miles to the northeast.

All these roads are made of stone, the limestone conglomerate being chiefly used to cover a good bed of granite well broken. In general, they are kept in ex-

MUHAMMADAN TOMB IN GUNTUR.

cellent repairs by the local fund department, a branch of the English government which looks toward self-government. Several large villages lie within a radius of about 12 miles. Mangalagiri, on the great northern road, is a town of over 6000 inhabitants. On a hill overlooking the town, there is a temple much frequented by pilgrims from all parts. It is believed by the natives that the image is accustomed to refuse to drink more than half its visitors offer! In the temple in the town there is a lofty tower of red sandstone, but by whom it was built is not determined. Among other villages of importance, we may mention Kaza, Vegendla, Prattipad, Potturu, Narakoduru and Rayapudi. Facing the Bay of Bengal on the south bank of the Krishna river, lies the

REPALLI TALUK,

which, owing to irrigation, is the most productive of all the seven Taluks. Its soil is a rich black alluvial deposit, a considerable portion of which lies below flood-tide, and must be protected from inundation by embankments. During the wet season, owing to the nature of the soil, the rice fields and the few good roads, the Taluk is almost impassable, and way must be made by means of the canals or along the narrow foot-paths which separate the rice fields; the latter is slow and often attended with great inconvenience. Attempts have been made to mix the black cotton soil and sand together, and thus improve the communicating roads, and with some success; but in the wet weather, it is a serious business to get a country cart through these roads without great delay and the exercise of a lot of patience. The canals which traverse the Taluk in different directions, form highways along which boats drawn by coolies may readily pass, but even then one cannot get around with that ease and facility which his work requires.

Sandole, Inturu, Nizampatam, on the bay near *Dindi Island*, Repalli, Kollur, Kolakaluru, Duggirala, and Tenali are large towns. Repalli is the seat of the Taluk government, and Tenali, a subdivision of the same. Duggirala is the centre of the canal system, four canals diverging therefrom. At Oleru there are the remains of a Roman Catholic Church, and in the last century, nearly the whole village was Roman Catholic. Sandole has a large Muhammadan population, and is a town of great antiquity, as many Buddhist remains show. The Hindu temple dates back to A. D. 1154. Ten miles from this place, across a dry sand belt, lies Nizampatam, near which Dindi Island is found, on which the Mission owns a large and two small bungalows, and over sixteen acres of land, some of which is covered with a very valuable cocoanut grove. The remaining Taluk to be noted is the

BAPATLA TALUK,

which lies south of Guntur. Its soil presents a great variety, a part is alluvial, part black cotton and red shale, and part covered by the sand ridge running along the coast. A canal traverses the Taluk from northeast to southwest, and irrigates a large part thereof. The non-deltaic parts are largely black cotton soil, which

TEMPLE TOWER AT BAPATLA.

68   AFTER FIFTY YEARS.

are apt to be flooded in the rainy season, and excessively dry in the hot, making it a very difficult field to work. Bapatla, with a population of 6000 is the seat of the

PALMYRA TOPE (GROVE) AT BAPATLA.

Taluk government, and has also one of the Munsiff's courts of the district. It is a flourishing town of considerable wealth and commercial importance. Near Bapatla are the large towns of Perala, Cheerala and Vetapalem, noted especially as centres of the weaving trade, where Hindu industry has to a remarkable degree held out against English goods.

Chebrole, nine miles southeast of Guntur, as its temple shows, dates back to the fourth century, the times of the Chola kings. Marco Polo, in A. D. 1290, landed on the coast of this Taluk. Peddi Ganzam, Santaravur, Karumchedu, Kommuru, Inkollu, Paturu, are large towns. At the first of these is the tidal lock, which ends the fresh and marks the beginning of the salt-water canal, which runs along the coast for two hundred miles to Madras, and is fed by backwaters from the bay.

From the subjoined table it appears that the area of the seven Taluks* is 4967 square miles, and the population in 1881, 904,016. In size our field is less than

*Taluk.	Area.	Population.	Villages.	Houses.
Bapatla	679	151,736	119	26,674
Repalli	644	184,340	154	31,415
Guntur	500	136,083	118	22,853
Narasarowpet	712	128,791	120	21,909
Palnad	1,057	125,799	100	24,356
Vinakonda	666	66,977	74	11,253
Satenapalli	714	110,290	188	18,752
Total	4,967	904,016	873	177,212

one-eighth that of Pennsylvania, while in density its population is twice as great. The people reside in 873 towns and villages, and occupy 177,212 houses. By the late census (1891) the population to the square mile is 224, that of Pennsylvania in 1880 was 95. But this with our western notions of houses conveys no idea of crowded condition of the hamlets. It must be remembered that all or nearly all the houses are *one story*, and have in many cases only *one room*. In many of the hamlets, as there is no place for extension to make room for the natural increase of population, the Government is taking vigorous steps to provide larger sites for congested villages. This crowded condition is especially observed among the outcastes.

The subjoined table* may prove of interest to those who would care to know how the people employ their time, and what proportion is engaged in the various callings. It will be noted with surprise that over fifty per cent. of the whole population are put down under

*Taluk.	Profession.	Domestic.	Commercial.	Agricultural.	Industrial.	Non-productive.
Bapatla	2,604	564	2,219	45,528	20,801	80,020
Repalli	2,402	464	2,350	60,063	17,127	101,934
Guntur	2,494	559	2,041	38,557	17,129	75,303
Narasarowpet	1,957	264	1,585	38,999	11,486	74,500
Vinakonda	769	94	1,114	20,432	6,153	38,413
Palnad	1,221	248	1,680	49,203	12,976	60,471
Satenapalli	1,276	70	1,174	37,078	11,822	58,834
Total	12,723	2,263	12,163	289,860	97,494	489,475

the head non-productive. This large army feeds on the laborer. But already we have spent too much time over the description of our present field.

We cannot turn away, however, to other matter without calling attention to new districts that are opening to us west and south in the Nellore district. Already a fair start has been made in this field, which gives promise of large accessions in the near future, if the work can be vigorously pushed and efficiently manned.

CHAPTER III.

OUR FIELD CONTINUED.

To the north of the Krishna lies the Godavery district, in many respects similar to the former, in wealth and productiveness, superior. Washed by the great Godavery river, from which one of the largest systems of irrigation is supplied, with a large delta of alluvial soil marvelous in richness, the district occupies a front place among those of this southern presidency. Its chief town and seat of government is Cocanada, on the Bay of Bengal, a place of considerable commercial activity. But the town in which our interests as a Mission centre is *Rajahmundry*. Although the Mission is no longer under the General Synod, it is quite in place, on account of its past relation, to refer to the founding and the subsequent handing over of the Mission to us, and by us to the General Council. The date of the starting of the Mission by the North German Missionary Society has been differently stated, but the best authorities agree that the work was commenced in 1843 by the Rev. L. M. Valett. Revs. Grönning and Heise joined the Mission in 1846, the former began work at Ellore, the latter remained in Rajahmundry. They at once started schools at both places, in which Telugu and English were taught, and which were especially intended for evangelistic purposes. Owing to severe financial troubles in Germany in 1851, the North German Society, much against its will, but because of the lack of funds and other work, deemed of greater importance, was compelled to close this work, but they did not wholly abandon the field, until they had provided for its continuance, by transferring it to the American Lutheran Missionary Society. Referring to this transfer in its report in 1853, the Society makes it the ground of a most earnest appeal for more men and means. By the transfer two men, the Revs. Heise and Valett, and considerable property, were placed at the disposal of the American Society. There were then two stations, Rajamundry and Ellore, but owing to Rev. Grönning's transfer to Guntur, the Ellore station was abandoned, though it was temporarily occupied by Rev. Martz, until his return to America in 1851. The offer to transfer this work was made in 1850, and in September of the same year, it was submitted to the churches. So prompt and favorable were the responses, that at a meeting in October of the same year, the transfer was completed.

The Rev. C. H. Schmidt says that the transfer was made on the express condition that the field be ever kept in connection with the Lutheran Church. Although no reference is found to this condition in the report of the committee to the General Synod in 1843, it subsequently turned out that, upon representations that such a condition was made, the Church Missionary Society handed back the field to the General Synod's committee, and they in turn, handed the work over to the General Council, or rather to the Missionary Society of those Synods which subsequently formed that general body. It is not necessary to enter into details of the causes which led to the relinquishment of this field by the General Synod's committee. It will suffice to say that principal among other causes were the rupture of the General Synod in 1866, the lack of men and means, and the growth of the Guntur and Palnad stations, requiring all the attention of the small staff of Foreign Missionaries. The Rev. E. Unangst was the *only man* in the field from 1866 to 1870. It is not to be wondered at that he was ready to hand this work over to any one who would undertake it. "In Missions among the Telugus," the writer seems inclined, without a knowledge of all the facts, to reflect somewhat on the Rev. Unangst for his part in the transfer to the Church Missionary Society. It may not be out of place to let him speak for himself. He says, as to the transferring (of the Rajahmundry field) in direct violation of the solemn promise made to the North German Society, "there was at that time nothing known to me of such a promise. The secretary of the executive committee made no allusion to such a promise in his letters to me, when the transfer was under consideration. My proposition was that the transfer be made to some other evangelical Mission, whose mode of work did not materially differ from ours. After consulting H. Morris, Esq., judge at Rajahmundry, a warm friend of our Mission, and a staunch supporter of the Church Missionary Society, I suggested the latter society as one of their stations. Ellore was near."

There was no intentional "quiet" observed in these transfer negotiations. The whole matter rested with the executive committee, and its secretary made no secret of the matter, so far as I can remember. But to say the *General Synod* was ready to do this, (viz., hand over this work), is a gratuitous statement. It was the executive committee that undertook the transfer, and it may be granted that the General Synod would have endorsed its action, and that is all it can be charged with. Everything was done fairly and squarely, without any idea whatever of subjecting the Lutheran Church to a disgraceful "humiliation." The transfer was to be made in good faith. But when the Pennsylvania Synod took up the matter, its proposition was acceded to "decently and in order." So far Dr. Unangst; and he was on the ground. Necessity was on him to look after the work. Already he had more than he could do at Guntur. Rajahmundry was 100 miles away. He could only entrust that work to those nearer. This he did, nothing more, nothing less. We only wonder he did not lose heart in the Church which could leave him single-handed for over four years, often without money too, and betake himself to some other fold. But though inducements were held out to him to enter the Church

Missionary Society, he stood alone, and maintained our work under circumstances which would have discouraged a more timid soul. The records of the Rajahmundry field show that the General Synod had charge of that work over eighteen years. During this time the men who carried on the work there were the Revs. Heyer, Grönning, Cutter, Long and Unangst. The Revs. Grönning and Heise remained in the Mission after its transfer to the American Lutheran Church; the former, however, labored at Guntur from 1850–62, finally retiring to Germany in 1865, while the latter continued at Rajahmundry till compelled by ill health to leave in 1862.

The Rev. Heyer's first connection with the Rajahmundry field was in 1854. In the minutes of the third annual meeting of the " Synod of the Lutheran Church in India," Father Heyer is referred to as absent, as he had shortly before moved to Rajahmundry. The Rev. Cutter remained in the field till 1855, when the ill health of his wife compelled him to return to America. The Rev. Long did noble service at Rajahmundry. Having opened the new station of Samulcotta, he labored for eight years (till he fell a victim to smallpox) with great zeal and success in this part of our field. He was never stationed at Guntur, but was at the last meeting of Synod at that place in 1859. He was an earnest, faithful soul loyal to his Master and the Master's work, and he performed a noble service for the church and India. Had he been more regardful of his own health, humanly speaking, he might have lived longer to labor for his Master. But as he was not impressed with the importance of vaccination, even rather opposed to it, holding that such precautions looked too much like a lack of faith in God, so when he fell sick, the disease found easy work in his system, which had already been weakened by eight years residence under a tropical sun. Along with this heavy grief, Mrs. Long was called upon to bear, within two weeks, the loss of her son and youngest daughter, by the same fell disease.

With the death of the Rev. Long the Mission was left entirely on the hands of one man, the Rev. E. Unangst. And what a struggle it was to keep on the work! Living at Guntur he exerted his utmost endeavors to conserve the work and hold the field for his beloved Church. But matters did not look hopeful in the home Church. The Fort Wayne conflict had rent the General Synod in twain. The interests of foreign missions were stifled in the fierce conflict of contending parties, and the lone missionary was left to fight his battles in far off India, without the support of the rear guard. It is hardly fair for any one even to intimate that he was disloyal to his Church. But if the real cause be sought on account of which he was ready to hand over the Rajamundry field, it must be found in his recognition of the fact that he could not work it from Guntur, that he had more to do at Guntur than he could possibly accomplish with the means at his command, and that the Church, in its disturbed condition, was failing to come up to her responsibility in the matter and was not sending reinforcements when they were absolutely essential to the life and progress of the Mission.

But we must point out that his plan to transfer the Rajahmundry field to the Church Missionary Society was not such an unusual step after all under the circumstances, for whilst he was considering the question with his Christian friend in India, the committee at home was brought to the same conclusion, and their letters to each other passed in mid-ocean. The secretary, the Rev. A. C. Wedekind, D. D., had written to the missionary in charge that he should try to negotiate a transfer to some Evangelical Society apparently unconscious, as was the missionary, that there was a condition that it was to remain forever a Lutheran Mission. It must be said to the credit of all parties concerned, that so soon as the Church Missionary Society was informed through the home committee of the Lutheran Society that such a condition existed, although their missionaries had been for some time in charge of the work, it was at once handed back to the Lutheran committee by the Rev. Alexander, who had been put in charge, pending final negotiations.

It is a matter of interest to note what was transferred to the General Council's Mission. All property received from the North German Society, and the addition of that made at Samulcotta were handed over. The church at that time numbered fifty-four communicant members. There were two central stations, six out-stations, a boys' boarding school—the result of twenty-seven years of labor, came into the hands of the new society. To take up this work the founder of the Mission, Father Heyer, nearing the borderland, three score and ten, came out, and until he saw the work safely entrusted to the hands of the Rev. H. C. Schmidt, held the Mission together, a fitting close to his heroic Indian career. It would be interesting to follow this work to the present, but as it no longer strictly belongs to our Mission, and as it has been made the subject of a little book, "Missions among the Telugus," we must pass on, referring the reader to it for fuller information. Suffice it to say, the Lord has greatly prospered the work, raised up faithful men and women to carry it forward, deemed some of them worthy of laying down their lives for the work, and out of trials and afflictions, built up a vigorous church numbering over 4000 adherents, of whom over 1000 are communicants.

CHAPTER IV.

THE MISSION'S FOREIGN STAFF.

Heyer, Gunn, Martz, Grönning, Heise, Snyder, Cutter, Long.

THE staff of foreign workers, its continuity, efficiency, zeal and energy, are matters of the first importance in such a work as this. Our Mission has been blessed with an earnest and devoted body of men and women, whose labors have been honored of God, and have been a blessing to the Hindu people. Our field is isolated. The people, largely cut off from the influence of the great centres of population, comparatively speaking, do not entertain such advanced ideas as are found in the larger towns and cities, which in a thousand ways have felt the sweep of western life and civilization. Consequently, the customs and habits of their fathers, the traditions of the elders, are more deeply rooted.

It was certainly no little undertaking for our first missionary to begin work in the midst of a people all of whom were going after other gods, and with a few followers, to plant a church in the wilderness. Doubtless the prophet's words kept ringing in his ears: "The desert shall rejoice and blossom as the rose, for in the wilderness shall waters break out, and streams in the deserts." God was leading then, as always, and though the way was hard and progress slow, these days of beginning were days of blessings from the presence of the Lord.

Our staff has always been small, too small to carry on the work successfully. It began with one lone toiler, Father Heyer, who two years later was cheered by the arrival of Rev. Gunn. It reached its maximum during the first fifty years in 1853, when there were five foreign missionaries, with their wives in the field. It was reduced to one in the years 1866–70 and in 1883, and again in 1887–90 to two men, though during the latter period there were two lady missionaries. It was never what it should have been. Undermanned, the Mission has always been, and never so much so as during the last ten years, wherein the work has grown so rapidly in all directions, that the "care of the churches" grows to be a great task. It has lately been strengthened by the addition of three new workers, yet our present staff of seven male and four female workers from the home church is small, nay, insignificant, when the great work to be done, as well as the varied work now being carried forward is remembered.

The following list shows the men and women who have labored in the Mission, and their time of service. The list is correct up to May, 1894.

NAME.	DATE OF JOINING.	LENGTH OF FURLOUGHS.	LENGTH OF FOREIGN SERVICE.	DATE OF LEAVING WITH CAUSE OR OF DEATH.
Rev. C. F. Heyer	Arrived in Guntur, July 31, 1842.	Furlough 1846-7. Returned Dec. 17, 1847. Retired 1857. Returned to Rajahmundry 1869. Retired finally 1871.	About 15 years.	Ill health caused him to withdraw in 1857. Old age in 1871.
Rev. Walter Gunn	Arrived June 18, 1844.	....	Over 7 years.	Died of consumption, July 5, 1851.
Mrs. Gunn	Arrived June 18, 1844.	....	....	Severed her connection finally in 1858.
Rev. G. J. Martz	Arrived Oct. 6, 1849.	....	Over 2 years.	Ill health. Returned 1852.
Rev. C. W. Grönning	Joined the Rajahmundry Mission, North German Society, July 22, 1846.	1858 April—25 Feb., 1861.	Over 17 years.	Ill health. Retired September 22, 1865.
Mrs. Grönning	November 8, 1850.	1858 April—25 Feb., 1861.	Over 13 years.	Ill health. Retired September 22, 1865.

NAME.	DATE OF JOINING.	LENGTH OF FURLOUGHS.	LENGTH OF FOREIGN SERVICE.	DATE OF LEAVING WITH CAUSE OR OF DEATH.
Rev. Heise	Same as Rev. Grönning.	1856.	About 16 years.	
Rev. W. E. Snyder	Arrived Madras January 23, 1852.	1856–58, April 1.	About 6 years.	Died March 5, 1859.
Mrs. Snyder (First Wife)	Arrived Madras January 23, 1852.		Over 2 years.	Died Sept. 3, 1854.
Mrs. Snyder (Second Wife)	Arrived April 1, 1858.		One year.	Retired latter part of 1859.
Rev. Wm. I. Cutter	Arrived Jan. 23, 1852.		Three years.	Retired to America.
Mrs. Cutter	Arrived Jan. 23, 1852.		Three years.	Ill health, Dec., 1855.
Rev. A. Long	Arrived Rajahmundry, March, 1858, while under Gen. Synod.		Eight years.	Died March 5, 1866.
Mrs. Long	Arrived Rajahmundry, March, 1858, while under Gen. Synod.		Eight years.	Retired from field November 8, 1866.

NAME.	DATE OF JOINING.	LENGTH OF FURLOUGHS.	LENGTH OF FOREIGN SERVICE.	DATE OF LEAVING WITH CAUSE OR OF DEATH.
Rev. E. Unangst, D. D.	Arrived April 1, 1858.	May 7, 1871—April 1, 1872.	Nearly 33 years.	Still at work.
Mrs. E. Unangst	Arrived April 1, 1858.	May 7, 1871 — Nov. 29, 1883.	About 18 years.	Died Feb. 16, 1888.
Rev. J. H. Harpster	Arrived at Guntur, April 1, 1872.	March 22, 1876. Active pastorate till Oct. 1, 1893. Returned Dec. 16, 1893.	Four years, first service.	In the field.
Mrs. J. H. Harpster	Arrived Dec. 16, 1893.			In the field.
Rev. L. L. Uhl, Ph.D.	Arrived Mar. 26, 1873.	March 16, 1885—Jan. 18, 1890.	Sixteen years.	In the field.
Mrs. L. L. Uhl	Arrived Mar. 26, 1873.	March 16, 1885.	Twelve years.	At home.
Rev. A. D. Rowe	December 11, 1874.	March 29, 1880 — Nov. 23, 1881.	Over 6 years.	Died Sept. 16, 1882.
Mrs. A. D. Rowe	December 11, 1874.	March 29, 1880 — Nov. 23, 1881.	Over 6 years.	Retired to America.

THE MISSION'S FOREIGN STAFF. 85

NAME.	DATE OF JOINING.	LENGTH OF FURLOUGHS.	LENGTH OF FOREIGN SERVICE.	DATE OF LEAVING WITH CAUSE OR OF DEATH.
Rev. Chas. Schnure	February 15, 1881.	....	Over 4 years.	Ordered home April 1, 1885.
Mrs. Schnure	February 15, 1881.	....	Over 4 years.	Dismissed Sept., 1885.
Miss Kate Boggs ...... (The first missionary of the W. H. & F. M. Society.)	February 15, 1881.	....	One year.	Ill health, etc., etc.
Rev. L. B. Wolf	November 29, 1883.	April 8, 1893.	Ten years.	At work.
Mrs. Wolf	November 29, 1883.	October 8, 1893.		At home.
Miss A. S. Kugler, M. D. .	November 29, 1883.	January 13, 1889—October 10, 1891. July 28, 1893—January, 1894.	Six years.	In work.
Miss F. M. Dryden	November 29, 1893.	February 13, 1891—October 10, 1891.	Nearly ten years.	In work.

Name.	Date of Joining.	Length of Furloughs.	Length of Foreign Service.	Date of Leaving with Cause or of Death.
Rev. W. P. Swartz	Arrived Oct. 14, 1885.	……	Over one year.	Retired Jan. 24, 1887.
Rev. John Nichols	January 30, 1886.	……	Less than one year.	Died Dec. 16, 1886.
Mrs. Nichols	January 30, 1886.	……	……	Retired Jan. 24, 1887.
Miss Susan Kistler	December 1, 1888.	……	Five years.	In work.
Rev. John Aberly	January 18, 1890.	February 24, 1894.	Over four years.	In work.
Mrs Aberly	January 18, 1890.	……	Over four years.	In work.
Miss Amy Sadtler	January 18, 1890.	February 24, 1894.	Over four years.	At home.
Rev. Geo. Albrecht, Ph.D.	October 23, 1892.	……	Over one year.	In work.
Rev. N. E. Yeiser	December, 1892.	……	Over one year.	In work.
Mrs. Yeiser	December, 1892.	……	Over one year.	In work.

It will be quite in place to refer at considerable length in this connection to those who have passed away, and to give a brief sketch of those still living. Our Mission founder,

THE REV. C. F. HEYER,

demands more than ordinary notice. A man of such apostolic zeal, whose name still lingers like a sweet benediction on the Mission, who was instrumental, in God's hands, of leading many souls to the light, and who earned by his work here and in America, the title "*an ideal missionary*," well deserves the consideration of his fellowmen, and the loving tribute of posterity. Were he among us to-day, he would have no one speak of him in any other than the humblest terms, as one who tried to do his duty to his fellowmen and His Lord, and yet his example and singleness of aim stand out in such bold relief from the narrowness and selfishness of so many others, that we may well pause and learn of him, as he learned of Christ, how to live. He never selected what was easy. He had, it would seem, a passion for hard service. He was the man for the hour, and God used him, as he was willing to be used. This is the secret of his life, the spring of his action. His rugged nature stopped at no hardship.

He was born in Brunswick, at Helmstedt, July 10, 1793. At the early age of three, he began to attend the parochial school, where he early attained proficiency in French. When only fourteen years of age, he was interpreter to the German citizens of the place, during the occupation of his home city, by the French soldiers of Napoleon I. The beginning of 1807 he spent among the French soldiers; in August he set out for America. Arriving in Philadelphia he lived with his uncle and attended a select school.

He united with the Zion's Lutheran Church, of which Dr. Helmuth was then pastor, and became a member of the choir. In 1809, deeply impressed by a sermon of his pastor, he underwent a great spiritual change, and his religious life took a deeper and more serious turn. From this time he is found active in the Sunday-school as a teacher, and shortly after, under the preaching of Dr. J. C. Baker his pastor, he determined to enter the ministry, studying theology, first under Dr. Helmuth, and subsequently under Dr. Schaeffer, the former's associate. While parochial school-master, in 1813, he preached his first sermon in the Philadelphia almshouse, and began that career of usefulness and devotion, which ended only with his life. But being anxious to fit himself in the best possible manner for his holy calling, after preaching at different places occasionally, and in his own church, December 24, 1814, we find him turning his face toward his native land, there to continue his studies at Göttingen, during 1815–16. Returning to America early in 1817, he was licensed by the Ministerium of Pennsylvania at York, and appointed traveling missionary in northwestern Pennsylvania, with Meadville and Erie as the centres of his operations. The next year, he is found at work in Maryland and southwestern Pennsylvania, with Cumberland as his headquarters, traveling over five

REV. C. F. HEYER.

counties, and enduring great hardship in the wild and mountainous country. During 1819, he is again traveling in southern Ohio, Kentucky and Indiana, while from 1830-39, he discharges the duties of agent of the Sunday-school Union of the southern church, carrying forward a great work in the distribution of the tracts, preaching almost every day in the out-of-the-way places, organizing Sunday-schools, and doing an invaluable work in laying the foundation of the Lutheran Church in these parts through which he preached and labored. In 1837 he traversed the Mississippi valley and laid the foundations of more than fifty future organized mission churches.

But all this self-denying work was only preparatory to his greater work in foreign parts. Noble as had been his career up to this time, he was only laying the foundation for his more brilliant labors in the great world-field, far hence among the gentiles. Already the church had been awakened, in 1837, by the call of Rheinus from India and Gutzlaff from China. The sainted Schmucker, deeply interested in the great question of the evangelization of the Gentiles, in the Lutheran Observer of January 13, 1837, in transmitting the appeal of Rheinus for publication, writes: "It is with feeling of no ordinary interest that I transmit the enclosed appeal. * * * There seems something providential in the conjunction of circumstances, the appeal reaching the churches when they are filled with burning zeal and ripe for the enterprise." We have already observed how zealously this work was taken up. In 1839, the General Synod, having appointed Rev. Wm. Heilig, determined *forthwith* to begin the work, either co-operating with Rheinus and his co-laborers, or establishing an independent station in India. Although the society of the General Synod was somewhat discouraged by the failure to enlist all Germans in this good work, and by the resignation of their missionary, and although the death of Dr. Rheinus, and the subsequent re-uniting of his co-laborers with the Church Missionary Society, removed the immediate occasion for engaging in this work, yet in the spring of 1840, the self-denying home missionary of our sketch, then in his forty-seventh year, offered himself for foreign service, and received the appointment.

And now the independent character of the man appeared. The missionary society, in consultation with the American Board, determined to begin work among the Telugus of south India, with the further understanding that all business should be transacted through the same Board ; it, however, being no part of this plan to interfere with the development of the new Mission along Lutheran lines, though in connection with said Board. But in Dr. Morris' report to the General Synod in 1843, this plan was strenuously opposed and the plan abandoned. Meanwhile, however, our founder-missionary had settled the matter in his own mind. He feared complications and future trouble would arise from such a union. It did not seem to him best. He thought he might be trammelled in his work, and its development would not be so free or harmonious with his Lutheran conceptions, as if he were to be independent. He at once sent his resignation to the society, and offered himself to his Synod, the Pennsylvania, to begin work under its control. Although this Synod had co-operated in the organization of the General Synod, it was not now in connection with it, and along with some other synods, had maintained an independent missionary society, so that it was in a position to take up the proposition at once, and at a public meeting in Philadelphia in October, 1841, the Rev. C. F. Heyer received his official instructions, preached a missionary sermon from the words: *Arise, go unto Nineveh, that great city, and preach unto it the preaching that I bid thee*, and made every arrangement to leave for his foreign field, which he did on the 14th of October, sailing from Boston. Its report to the Synod by the missionary society sets forth the following conditions of his engagement:

1. "He should, as soon as he could get ready, go to East India, and begin the work at such place as the Lord would open a door for him.

2. "His traveling expenses should be paid by the committee.

3. "He shall receive a salary of six hundred dollars annually. Should he be able to get through with less, he promised to accept a smaller amount, over against which we promised that should the above sum not be sufficient to sustain him, we would give him more.

We also allowed him one hundred and fifty dollars for traveling expenses."

In the spring of 1842, he arrived at Columbo, Ceylon, and thence he traveled by land to Madras, visiting Palamcottah, Tranquebar and Tanjore, and arriving in Madras in the latter part of May. "In June and July," in his own words, "an exploring tour was undertaken with the intention of selecting a permanent place of residence." His search for a field led him into the Telugu country, where we have seen it was the original intention of the General Synod to labor in 1840. Keeping along the east, commonly called the Coromandel coast of the southern peninsula, he continued northward for two hundred and forty miles, until he reached Bapatla, a town of considerable size in the Krishna district. Pioneer in the western wilds of the United States, he attempted some things which in a tropical climate like India are extremely dangerous. But he soon learned that some things could be done in his former work, which were now impossible. His first tour from Madras to Bapatla, in a palankeen, in search of a field shows how little he consulted his own comfort. Having arrived at Bapatla, an event transpired which changed all his plans, and which secured him the support of the best friend in India the Mission ever had, H. Stokes, Esq., the collector and magistrate of the district. "Father Heyer" was accustomed to tie up his palankeen between the trees, and use it for a house when stopping during his journey. Thus he was found by Stokes. He at once enquired where the new missionary intended to live. Heyer said his house was yonder, pointing in the direction of two palmyra trees, to which, as usual, he had swung his palankeen. "But I see no house yonder," replied Stokes. "No, that is so, but I live in my palankeen," said Heyer. It did not take the practical Christian friend long to see through the simple devotion of this heroic soul. "Why," said he, "that will never do. You cannot live thus in such a country as this. You have not come here to die, but to live and work. Come and live with me till a house can be secured. I will arrange for a school-house and church by making some changes in my outbuildings, and you can begin your work." Here was God's hand at work through His faithful servant. Stokes knew the country, Heyer did not. "For six months," says the missionary, "I lived with this servant of God, and while I expected to have nothing but privation and self-denial in India, I soon found that with him and at his table, I was to live like a prince. I was never more comfortably situated in my life."

July 31, 1842, we may regard as the birthday of our Mission, as it was on this day that Heyer arrived in Guntur, and took up his residence with Collector Stokes. However, though as seen, he was thus comfortably situated, there never was a man less given to thought about his bodily comforts. Indeed he did not take sufficient care of himself and, as a consequence, he had only fairly entered on his work when his health gave way, and he was compelled to seek a change by a furlough to America. But this did not take place until the missionary was permitted to see the fruits of his labors in the baptism of a number of souls. Beginning his work under the guidance, and with the faithful assistance of his friend Stokes (this was before the mutiny and the religious non-interference policy of the British government), he soon saw the vastness of the task, and began to realize that a mighty struggle must be made, in which God had called him to strike some of the first blows. His first baptisms were the children of Christian servants who had followed their masters to Guntur, after having become converts to Christianity in other parts of India. But the debilitating climate was too much, even for that rugged frame which had endured over twenty years of pioneer work on the American frontier. He succumbed to the climate, prostrated by the great heat, and returned to America in 1846. But in the genial climate of his native land, he soon recovered his wonted health, and longed to be back at his post of duty. While he was home, the Rev. Walter Gunn, who had been sent out by the General Synod's executive committee, carried on the work. The work was now under the control of this Synod, and when Rev. Heyer's health was sufficiently recovered to allow his return, he offered his services to the committee, which were gladly accepted, and after visiting many of the churches in the interest of the Mission, and urging its claims and needs, he left America the second time, on December 4, 1847, and arrived in Madras, March 16, 1848. On his return, he was pained to see the seeds of consumption gradually undermining the health of his noble colleague. It should be noted, that though he returned under the auspices of the General Synod's committee, he still held his accustomed relations toward the Ministerium of Pennsylvania, and sent annual reports of his work to that body. This the committee readily acceded to, and no trouble, ecclesiastical, interfered with the good work. In fact, there was little occasion, inasmuch as the old Synod was back in the General Synod a few years after this arrangement with the missionary.

Already, in 1843, the Revs. Heyer and Vallet, of the North German Society, had made a tour of inspection through the Palnad Taluk, which was destined to be the scene of Father Heyer's greatest triumphs. During this tour the truth took root, at least, in one heart, and from it, early in 1847, we can trace the first baptism in this fruitful field. Again his old friend Stokes came to his assistance, by presenting the missionary with a bungalow and lot at Gurzal. During his first year's residence in his new field, thirty-nine persons were baptized. It was when he began his work here, that we again see the true character of the man, his fearlessness and devotion to duty. His new field was in the most malarious part of the district, and few, if any Europeans, had lived there before his time. But nothing deterred, he made all preparations for the worst. Bidding good-bye to his friends at Guntur, on arriving in the Palnad, he prepared for death, got his grave dug, and made every possible arrangement in case he took the deadly fever. Surely death never moved him from his purpose. And when in God's good time, after he had lived and triumphed over all his fears, notwithstanding the climate and deadly fevers, as he leaves this field, the scene of his many labors and faithful toil, there is something truly apostolic and sublime to hear him say, as he stands by that open grave, which he had been quite ready to fill, if God so willed, "Oh grave, I have conquered thee; I have robbed thee of thy spoil; to God be all the glory. Amen."

He laid the foundation of our Palnad Mission during his residence there, from 1849 to 1853. His labors here were of a most self-denying character. Without the least thought of himself, he lived such a life of self-denial as to vie with the fakirs and sanyasis of India. In fact he is still looked upon as a great saint, and his name is still remembered in his old field of labor.

But he had feelings too, and his German spirit and temper got the better of him as the following shows. On one occasion, when his palankeen bearers did not turn up at the time ordered, he was seen striding angrily toward the village, and shortly returned brandishing his cane in the fiercest manner possible, and driving the whole lot of bearers before him into the compound; a rather unmissionary performance it may be thought by some, and yet one to which a set of Indian bearers could drive a Job himself!

It was on another occasion that he used his cane upon one of his members who was disposed, on account of caste prejudices, to make trouble, and thus tried by a bit of "muscular" Christianity to force men from those deeply rooted customs and beliefs, which after all only time and God's grace through the ages will change. But with all this, he was a *father* among the people. Impulsive, generous, kind, patient, nothing was too burdensome for him to undertake, nothing too humble, if he could win a soul.

In 1853, his health again becoming very much impaired, and thinking a change to Guntur would be beneficial, at the close of the year he exchanged fields of labor with the Rev. Grönning. From the minutes of the "Lutheran Synod in India," we learn that he was transferred to Rajahmundry at the close of 1854, and was not present at the meeting of the synod in February, 1855. After his transfer to Guntur, he enjoyed good health during the year 1854. At the third meeting of the synod, the president in his official report remarks on the health of the missionaries, and says that "all had suffered greatly except Brother Heyer." But his days in India were rapidly drawing to a close. He was growing old, and the infirmities of age, under a most debilitating climate, made it hard for him to continue his arduous work. All his life, as we have seen, had been more or less one of exposure, and rugged though his frame was, it began to show signs of weakness. Already in 1853, when our sainted friend Mr. Stokes refers to him, he speaks of his failing health, and that he cannot long continue at his post. At the close of 1857 it became manifest that he would have to leave his work. This he was very reluctantly forced to do. Leaving India at the close of 1857, we find him no sooner at home than, filled with his old spirit of self-denial, he again offers himself for home mission service. He was a pioneer, and such he was determined to be to the end.

From 1858 to 1868 he worked in the great northwest, doing a missionary work which resulted in the formation of the Minnesota Synod, which he represented in the General Synod in 1864 and 1866, and subsequently in the Council.

But again the old hero shows his character. During the pending of negotiations relative to the transfer of the Rajahmundry field to the Church Missionary Society, he had gone to Germany. While there, he heard of the proposed transfer. His soul was fired at once with his old zeal and love in the foreign cause. "We must keep this work in the Lutheran Church." Taking counsel with Pastor Grönning, they determined on a course of action. Candidate Schmidt, who was then studying under Grönning, was to accompany Father Heyer to America. He was to be further prepared, and then ordained for the work. Meanwhile, Father Heyer was to return to India, and set matters right over there. Correspondence was at once begun with the executive committee of the General Synod, with a view to avert the transfer, and secure the field for the Lutheran Church, as represented by the Pennsylvania Synod. All parties agreed to this new proposal. The Church Missionary Society, as has been shown, readily acquiesced in the request. It was a touching sight to see the old man, now almost seventy-seven years of age, appearing on the floor of the synod, and pleading for his work, offering to go and stay at this crisis until a young man could be prepared to assume the responsibility. Here again we find him, conferring not with flesh and blood, seeing only the work of his Master, and ready to go to the ends of the earth to do his bidding. Has this fire departed? Is such faith, earnestness and devotion no more found in the Church?

With a grip in hand, on August 31, 1869, he started to India for the third time, and before the Rev. Unangst knew what had happened, one day in December, as from the clouds, "Father Heyer" dropped down upon him. How overjoyed were they to see him! With what interest he examined the work, and noted the signs of progress during the decade of his absence! How with tears of joy he beheld what God had wrought! The total baptisms at the close of his service in the whole field had been 196. When he returned they had increased to 858, and a vigorous work was seen on all sides.

The old hero's ideas of sacrifice are the same. It is both pathetic and amusing to hear how he came into the Mission compound on his return, and on seeing the new bungalow which the missionary had built when the doctor declared that the old one was too unhealthy to be occupied, exclaimed with astonishment, "Whose house is this? What king built it?" Then, calling out to Dr. Unangst, he repeated the soliloquy for his benefit. When he saw Mrs. Unangst and the children, and observed in what wretched health the former was, on account of a residence of almost twelve years, tears came to his eyes, and he urged their return to America.

After spending a few days and revisiting his old friends, he proceeded to Rajahmundry and took up the work there, which he found in a very sadly disorganized condition. Arriving there, December 1, 1869, he began to gather the scattered flock, and during his first year he baptized 107, and administered the holy communion to those who had remained faithful. In February, 1870, he was strengthened by the accession of the Rev. Becker, but in three months he succumbed to the climate, and left the old hero alone again. But this misfortune was of short duration. No sooner had this workman fallen, than God raised up another, who has made full proof of his call to India. The Rev. C. H. Schmidt was on his way to India, spending some time in Germany. But on hearing of the death of Becker, he hastened to India by the overland route, and arrived in Rajahmundry August 4, 1870, to the great joy of Father Heyer.

He had done what he promised to do, and though

urged to remain in India a year longer, the infirmities of age and urgent family affairs compelled him to sever his connection with the work he loved so well. Leaving India at the close of 1870, after a service of fourteen months, he spent the closing days of his life as house father and chaplain in the Lutheran Theological Seminary at Philadelphia. Here he lived, and honored by students and professors, he passed away to his eternal rest after an illness of eleven days, on the 7th of November, 1873, in the eighty-first year of his age.

So closed the life of one of God's noblemen, who did a work both at home and abroad in founding the Church of Christ which cannot be estimated. God only knows the vast reach and the true value of his labors. It were easy to eulogize such a character. But his work and sacrifice for the master need no eulogy. Like Abou Ben Adhem, his name is written among the names of those who loved their fellowmen. His life is a rich legacy to his Church and to her children. We should be thankful for it. His work remains, nay has grown in volume and importance, and men of his spirit are still needed to carry it on. The Church has the men, and Heyer's work calls upon her to send them into the field, "white unto the harvest." Sacrifice of a high order is still needed, and he calls, by his self-sacrificing life, upon men to deny themselves, and take up the work, in the doing of which the Master will be honored, and the kingdom of peace and blessedness established among men.

THE REV. WALTER GUNN,

born at Carlisle, Schoharie county, New York, June 27, 1815, spent his early years amid poverty. After being convinced of the truth his mind was deeply interested in the condition of the heathen world, and he determined, if possible, to fit himself for foreign service. The Hartwick Synod, in 1837, resolved to assist him in making his preparations, and with the help of the Mrs. Schafler, Crouse, Senderling and Lintner, educated him, these efforts of the women being the first *organized* attempt to advance the cause of Foreign Missions in which the women of the Church engaged. After studying at an academy in his native county, he entered Union College, from which he graduated in 1840. His subsequent course of study was at the Theological Seminary at Gettysburg, where he graduated in 1842, the year in which Father Heyer founded the Mission at Guntur. Licensed by the Hartwick Synod, September 6, 1842, after assisting other ministers in special services at different places with great acceptance, he was appointed to the foreign field, May 25, 1843. After his marriage to Miss Pultz, and ordination at Johnstown by the Hartwick Synod, September 5th, 1843, he sailed for India the following November, arriving at Guntur, June 18, 1844. Having been instructed to co-operate with the Rev. Heyer, it is pleasant to note that he was received with open arms by that worthy and devoted soul, and they continued to labor harmoniously until the latter was compelled to withdraw for a time, and

104 AFTER FIFTY YEARS.

MRS. WALTER GUNN.

REV. WALTER GUNN.

the whole work was given into the hands of the former. After the usual first struggle with the language and endeavors to preach through an interpreter, always a most difficult as well as unsatisfactory undertaking, he was greatly rejoiced when he had made sufficient progress to be understood in their own language. Writing in the very house in which he lived and did his work, which he had built and in which he subsequently died, the writer has been able to appreciate some of the early scenes in this dear saint's life, for Gunn was one of God's most pious children. His letters home breathe the spirit of the deepest piety, and his hopes and desires, expressed in all his writing, show him to have been a man whose life was lived very close to God. A cyclone having destroyed his house in 1846, he had to superintend the erection of another. In 1847, he was left in sole charge of the Mission. He had four schools, and his Sunday congregation numbered from 50 to 150 attendants. How much, he says, "will spring up and bear fruit of the seed sown is known only to God in whom we trust."

When Heyer returned from America his determination to plant a station in the Palnad, in 1849, left Gunn again in sole charge of the Guntur field. Already his health had begun to decline. Attacks of fever were followed by seasons of general prostration, allowing him to exert himself very little. His physician urged him to seek relief in a change of climate. He went to Madras with his wife, for a time, and spent part of 1850, at the house of Dr. Scudder of the American Board. He seemed to find relief in this change, and returned to his work in June, 1850. But it soon became evident that the change for the better was only temporary. But though confined to his own room, he did not cease his work. Praying and talking with converts in his sick room, he could yet write to a friend of God's great mercies to him, since he had left his native land. "Three or four times," he continues, "I was within a step of death, but I am still alive * * * . I was thinking a few evenings since, what a privilege it was, in the midst of bodily weakness and languor, to listen to the fervent prayers of the converts * * * . It is delightful to meet with these first fruits around the throne of grace." While writing thus, he was steadily nearing the border-land. He lingered on, however, through the wet season of 1850, and up to the middle of 1851, growing weaker as the days passed away, but living in an atmosphere of spiritual exaltation, which it is beautiful to contemplate. When the end drew near, he resigned himself into God's hands, and spent much of his time in prayer. He comforted his sorrow-stricken wife with the divine assurances of God's Holy Word, and spent much time in reading, and when too weak, in having read to him, the Psalms. He had them read through each month. His favorite hymn was "Rock of Ages." On June 27th, his birthday, his colleague, Grönning visited him, and the day following he partook, for the last time, of the Holy Communion, surrounded by a few of his most intimate friends. The closing hours of his life were rapidly running out. Commending his wife and little ones to God, he prepared to depart hence. Up to this time he wanted to remain longer for his friends' sake, but shortly before he passed away a great change came over him, and with the words, "Yes, Jesus is with me," on his lips, he fell asleep without a struggle, and passed into that perfect peace beyond.

So passed away, July 5, 1851, from the midst of his labors, at the early age of thirty-six, one of those choice souls whom God has given for India's regeneration. His quiet and peaceful death was a rich benediction to those around. Cut down in the midst of his days, when the infant Mission was just fairly started, he entered into rest when, to human appearances, he was just fully equipped for his work. Though not a man of brilliant talents, he was held in high esteem by all who knew him, and for his sound advice he was worthy of the highest confidence. Humble, prayerful, conscientious, he was ever found at his post of duty, and when once he saw his duty his love for others, and for his Master, made him eager to perform it.

He was patient and persevering, two excellent traits in a foreign missionary, and his Christian example was a rich legacy to the Church he had helped to establish.

Looking over his diary, you find evidences on every page of that serious and deep earnestness which characterized his missionary career. In 1847, he made a tour through the western part of the field, a full account of which he sent to the secretary of the executive committee. He had pretty generally traveled over the whole of that territory now under our control, and was indefatigable in his labors. His schools engaged his most earnest attention, and he was greatly rejoiced to see the children brought under the influence of the gospel. In them he was wont to find his greatest hope. Speaking once of the discouragements of the work, he continues, "but to the eye of faith *there is encouragement;* the truth committed to memory from day to day * * * is the truth of God * * * A blessing will follow after many days." How prophetic these words were has been shown by the subsequent history of our progress. The seed sown in the school has produced a splendid harvest which is now being gathered, a harvest which is so abundant that it taxes the ability of the Mission to gather and properly garner it. But we pass to the next missionary,

THE REV. GEORGE J. MARTZ.

Educated at Gettysburg, in both college and seminary, he received his appointment as foreign missionary in 1849, being in his twenty-seventh year, having been born August 27, 1822. He early took a deep interest in the work of foreign missions, and as soon as the grave situation in India on account of Rev. Gunn's delicate health became known, he saw an opportunity to carry out his early desires, and offered himself for the work. Licensed by the Maryland Synod, October 18, 1848, upon his appointment to the foreign field, he was or-

REV. GEORGE J. MARTZ.

dained the following year, and sailed for India, April 19, 1849. After a long voyage in a sailing vessel around the Cape, he arrived in Madras, and on October 6, 1849, reached Guntur. Kindly greeted by the European officials of the station, among whom was the Mission's tried friend Collector Stokes, and warmly welcomed by the missionary band, he was soon at work studying the language and acquainting himself with his new surroundings. Rev. Heyer being at work in the Palnad, Rev. Gunn sick in Madras, he had sole charge for a time of the Guntur station. He preached his first sermon in Telugu with the assistance of his Munshi in translation, about a year after his arrival. After preaching in and around Guntur, he made a tour with Rev. Heyer in the Palnad, and began to contemplate the opening of a new station in the Nizam's dominions. But this idea was soon abandoned, both because the field was already large, and also was soon to be greatly extended by the addition of the Rajahmundry field of the North German Society. When this transfer was made, after Rev. Gunn's death, Rev. Grönning was transferred to Guntur, and Rev. Martz was stationed at Ellore, one of the out-stations of the Rajahmundry field. It was while there that his health failed, and he was compelled to leave his work, begun with so much promise, after less than two years of active service. He returned to America, and served as pastor at different places. He is still living and resides at Lebanon, Pennsylvania.

THE REV. C. W. GRÖNNING.

Of the two missionaries who were taken over in the transfer of the Rajahmundry field, one was the Rev. C. W. Grönning. He had already served the missionary cause over six years under the North German Society. Born in Denmark, at Fredricia, November 22, 1813, he was educated at Hamburg (1840-5), and left his native land for India, December 15, 1845, in company with the Rev. Heise. Landing at Calcutta, Whitsunday, 1846, he took a coasting vessel to Madras, and thence returned to Cocanada, arriving at Rajahmundry, July 22, 1846, seven months after leaving Germany. In 1849, he opened the new station of Ellore, which subsequently passed into the hands of the Church Missionary Society. His marriage to Miss Krug was solemnized in November, 1850. He moved to Guntur, and took charge of the work there, during the last illness of Gunn. In 1854 he was transferred to the Palnad and took charge of Father Heyer's work who, as we have seen, removed to Guntur on account of his failing health. In this arduous field he labored with great success. From March, 1858, to February 25, 1861, he was at home. At the end of this furlough of almost three years, he returned to Guntur and took up his old work in the Palnad and the Telugu work of the Guntur field. Owing to Rev. Heise's ill health and withdrawal, the Rajahmundry station becoming vacant, he proceeded to that field in March, 1862. It was during the great stringency in funds felt by the Mission, 1862-65, due to the

Civil War in America, that Rev. Grönning began to negotiate the transfer of the Rajahmundry field to some German society, and so far had the matter gone that he had written for re-inforcements, and received favorable responses, Rev. Mr. Mylius having joined him, with the promise of support from Germany. But the executive committee not approving of this plan of re-adjustment, Rev. Mylius soon sought other fields for his labors, founding what is now known as the Hermannsburg Mission of South India. Thus, though not in a regular way, this plan resulted in the furtherance of the gospel, and the establishment of a new centre of missionary influence. The missionary continued at Rajahmundry till 1865. Then God laid the heavy hand of affliction upon him, and he was called upon to mourn the death of his son Charles. This sad bereavement was too much for his wife's already impaired health, and rendered a change necessary to her native land. He was obliged to accompany his family; so after handing over his work to Rev. Long, who had removed from Samalcotta to Rajahmundry about this time, he left India, September 22, 1865, and finally severed his connection with the work after seventeen years of faithful service. However, though no longer actively engaged, his interest in the great cause continues, and his son, born in Guntur, lately returned to Rajahmundry and began his work with bright promise for the future, when suddenly he was called home, July 9, 1889, by India's terrible scourge—cholera—not, however, until he had shown himself a worthy scion of his missionary ancestry.

Missionary Grönning was soon at work in his native land. He served as pastor at Apenrade, and subsequently at Ballum Slesvic. He was decorated with the order of the Red Eagle by the Emperor of Germany, is now pensioned, and resides with his youngest son Herman, at Apenrade, where the latter is pastor. He was a man of strong character. When determined on a course of action, he would not easily yield to outside influence. His work was marked by his German determination. He saw the beginning of large accessions in the Palnad Taluk, the beginning of that victory of the cross, that reign which shall finally prevail over all men.

THE REV. HEISE

was co-laborer and fellow-countryman of Rev. Grönning. They came to India together in 1845, under the auspices of the North German Society. He came under the General Synod's executive committee along with the transfer in 1851. His work was entirely in connection with the Rajahmundry field, though he was frequently at Guntur, took part in the organization of the synod at Guntur in 1853, and was president of that body in 1858 at its Rajahmundry meeting. He was on leave in 1856, and married, returning with his wife to the work in 1857. He was very active in furthering the formation of a conference of *all Lutheran* missionaries with a view to form a joint synod. But in the midst of his work his health gave way, and in 1861, after sixteen years' service in India, ten of which were in connection with the General Synod's society, he relinquished his work, left the field, and severed his connection with the Mission. He was acting usher in the Keil University in 1862, and died shortly afterwards.

THE REV. WILLIAM E. SNYDER

was born in the year 1822 in the state of New Jersey. Educated at Hartwick Seminary, and subsequently at Rutgers College, he determined early in life to enter

REV. W. E. SNYDER

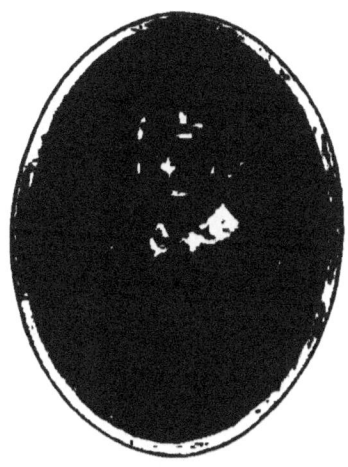
MRS. W. E. SNYDER.

the gospel ministry. His theological course was taken at Hartwick Seminary, at which place he spent several years as an assistant teacher in the school department, acquitting himself with credit. While there his mind became impressed with the great cause of Missions, and he determined to devote himself to that work.

Ordained by the Hartwick Synod in 1851, married to Miss St. John about the same time, he and his wife, with his fellow-missionary Rev. W. I. Cutter and his wife, sailed for India, August 11, 1851, and after a tedious voyage around the Cape of 165 days, reached Madras, January 23, 1852.

Having been appointed to the Guntur field, he shortly after this joined his post, and owing to his previous experience became very active in the schools of the Mission, especially the English school started at this station about this time. But his Indian career was destined to be both sad and short. When hardly fairly established, he was called on to mourn the loss of his beloved wife, who "fell on sleep" in Jesus, September, 1854, leaving an only child, Lottie, who was sent to America with the Cutters in 1855. Impaired health compelled him to go on furlough in 1856. While home he married again. His health being restored, he determined to return to his former work at Guntur, which was greatly needing his presence. Subsequently, in company with the Revs. Unangst and Long and their wives, he embarked for India, at Boston, November 23, 1857, just at the close of the Sepoy mutiny. His daughter returned with him to India. Detained at Masulipatam, the head station of the Church Missionary Society, fifty miles from Guntur, he did not arrive at Guntur till the end of April, 1858. We find him at once in the midst of his work, looking after the schools, preaching in the villages, and touring throughout the Guntur and Palnad fields. But in the midst of his usefulness and labors he was cut off. Hardly a year had passed after his return, when the end came like a flash out of the clear sky. After a long tour in the Palnad, under the influence of which he sent a most cheering report to the executive committee, he returned to Guntur, was seized by cholera, and in twelve hours had passed away, deeply mourned by his family and friends of the Mission, a great loss to the little band of missionaries. Thus on March 5, 1859, in the midst of his many labors, and the beginning of a most encouraging work, he laid down his weapons, ended his toil, and went to his reward and rest. After a little less than six years service for his Master, his place was left vacant in the Mission's councils and work. But his work is moving on. God never lets the death of a workman interfere with His plans, though men may think so. It often happens that when they think others most ripe for work, His thoughts are not man's. To Him who knows what is best and never makes mistakes, Missionary Snyder was ripe for eternity, and He took him and laid his work on others.

THE REV. WILLIAM I. CUTTER

was born in Germany, of Roman Catholic parents, July 29, 1820. He came with his parents to America in 1833. His academic education was received at schools in Kentucky, under Revs. Yeager and Kurtz, and his collegiate, at Wittenberg College, in the days of the sainted Keller. His theological training was received at Wittenberg College and Hartwick Seminary. He and his wife sailed for India, August 11, 1851. He was designated for the Rajahmundry field to join the Rev. Heise. Here he began work, and his wife organized, with the financial aid of her English friends, one of the

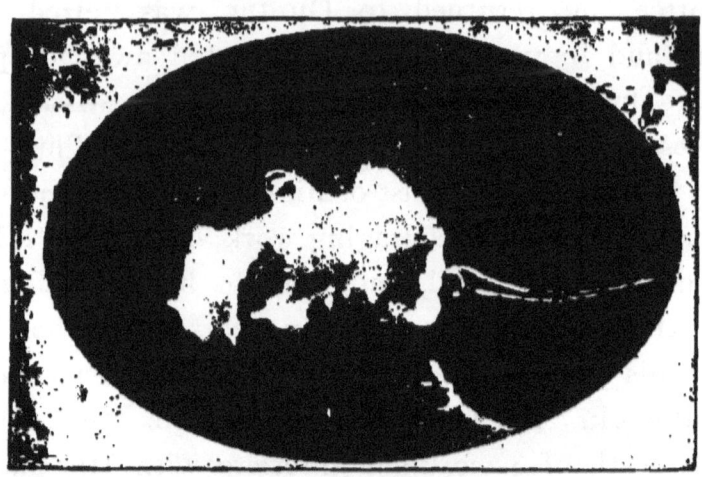

MRS. W. I. CUTTER.

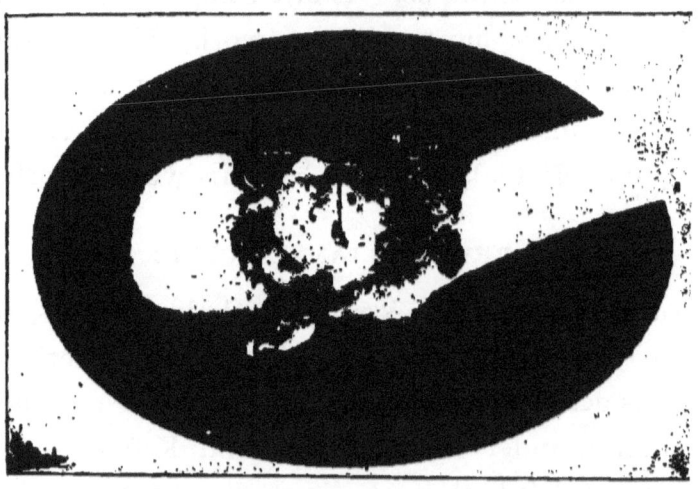

REV. W. I. CUTTER.

first schools *for girls* in our Mission at that place. Meanwhile orders came for him to remove to Guntur to relieve Grönning, but the continued ill health of his wife made it impossible for her to remain in India. So that in December, 1855, he was forced to quit his post and sever his connection with the Mission, but not his interest. In a personal interview with him at his home in Atchison, the writer was struck with his earnestness in and love for the work.

THE REV. ADAM LONG,

born December 14, 1825, in Clarion Co., Pa., received his academic instruction at Zelienople, and graduated at Pennsylvania College, Gettysburg, with the class of 1854, and subsequently at the seminary at the same place. He received his appointment from the executive committee early in 1857, intending to join his field in the early summer of the same year; but owing to the disturbed state of India, due to the Sepoy Mutiny, he did not leave America until the end of the year, in company with Revs. Unangst and Snyder, arriving in his field early in April, 1858. He was designated to the Rajahmundry field, but at once, under the instructions of the India Synod, he determined to open a new station, and after consultation, selected Samalcotta, a town about thirty miles from Rajahmundry. Here he labored with great zeal and encouraging results from the date of his opening the station until he was called to Rajahmundry, by the failing health of Grönning, to undertake the work at the head station. This was in 1865, and from that time he had sole charge of the Rajahmundry work.

He was present at the meeting of the India Synod at

Rajahmundry in 1858, at its meeting in 1859 at Guntur, and he reported the opening of the Samalcotta station to the executive committee at this time. In 1859, there

REV. & MRS. ADAM LONG.

were only two men present, Unangst and Long. Heise was detained at home by sickness, and Grönning was on furlough.

But the worst was yet to come. No sooner had the Mission been deprived of the valuable services of Grönning and Heise (we have noticed the withdrawal of these workers, and the removal of Long to Rajahmundry in 1865), than it was called upon to mourn the sudden death of Long. Having taken charge of Rajahmundry from Grönning, September, 1865, he was the only missionary in that part of the field. While busy at his work he fell a victim to smallpox, and on March 5, 1866, after almost eight years of faithful service, when the work was so full of promise, and stood, humanly speaking, so much in need of him, he was called hence to his eternal reward. His second child, a son, and youngest, a daughter, died of the same fell disease, within two weeks of each other and of his own death. It was a heavy stroke for his wife and the Mission. It looked like the death-blow of the work as well. In 1865, Grönning was compelled to withdraw, and Long falling at his post, *one lone missionary* is left to carry on the work—all seemed to conspire against its continuance. It was a dark day.

And what made matters worse, Fort Wayne had disorganized the home forces; the men promised by Grönning from Germany could not be sent for want of funds. The cause was in a sad state. It looked as if the recent sad divisions in the Church, together with the distractions attending them, would result in the total failure of the Mission, when "efforts to reinforce Unangst" in India had proved fruitless. But though Long died, and the cause languished for want of home support, the Lord of the harvest kept watch over His work. He watched the growth of this tree of His own planting, when the friends of the cause slept or were at other business. He brought the Mission out of this narrow strait into a broad place, set it upon its feet, and established its goings. Blessed be His holy name! Amen.

CHAPTER V.

FOREIGN STAFF CONTINUED.

Unangst, Harpster, Uhl, Rowe, Schnure, Boggs, Wolf, Kugler, Dryden, Swartz, Nichols, Kistler, Aberly, Sadtler, Albrecht, Yeiser.

THE Rev. Erias Unangst, D. D., the senior missionary of our foreign staff, was born in Lehigh Valley, Pa., August 8, 1824. His classical and theological training was received at Gettysburg, where he spent some time as tutor in the Preparatory School. Ordained by the Alleghany Synod in 1857 while under appointment, married in September of the same year, he sailed for India, November 23, 1857, when the news of the Sepoy mutiny filled all hearts with fear. Arriving at Guntur, April 1, 1858, he began to study the language, and on the death of Snyder took charge of the schools, and on the return of Grönning divided the field and work with him. He was honored with the doctorate by Wittenburg College in 1878. He has served on the committee of the revision of the Telugu translation of the Bible for many years. Through the death and withdrawal of his fellow missionaries, he was left in sole charge of the whole Mission from 1866 to 1870, until the return of Heyer in December, 1869, who took charge of the

FOREIGN STAFF CONTINUED.

MRS. E. UNANGST.

REV. E. UNANGST, D. D.

Rajahmundry field for the General Council. He has seen the Mission in all its phases; its best and darkest days are alike familiar to him. In 1871, May 7th, after thirteen years of uninterrupted labor, he proceeded on furlough to America with his family; but such were the exigencies of the work that he remained home only about nine months. While absent there was no American missionary in the field and the work was carried on by Mr. Cully, a Eurasian, as an Evangelist, who had entered the Mission in 1862 under Grönning in connection with his Palnad work. After an absence of less than a year from the field, he returned April 1, 1872, leaving his wife and family in America. This great sacrifice of separation from his loved ones he bravely bore for ten years, until the Church almost forgot the fact. In 1882 he again went on furlough, but scarcely had he reached home when the death of Rowe made it imperative that he should return at once. This he did, with his wife and daughter Ellenora; leaving Philadelphia August 25, 1883, and reaching his old field in November of the same year. While in America he was called to mourn the death of his father and one of his sons. Since his return he has lost his faithful wife, who "fell on sleep," February 16, 1888, while he was absent in the Palnad. Of his large family only two remain, but he continues his work amid the sunshine and shadows of life, serving his King; quietly, steadily carrying on his work, confident that the end of his labors shall be blessed. For more than thirty-five years he has borne the heat and burden of this Indian work, until this, his adopted home, has grown dearer to him than his native land,

REV. E. UNANGST, D. D. IN HIS STUDY.

and hardly a wish escapes him for the land of his birth. His is an Indian cast of mind and way of working. His movements are Indian—indeed, to hear him talk there is no place in which he would rather live and labor than India. Over three score and ten, his bow abideth in strength and he can endure a pretty hard lot of touring yet. But as he is living, and his modesty would not allow a remark to be made about him which would lead men to think that he was in the least bit doing anything more than the ordinary, we desist, with the wish, however, that he may be long spared to this work, to which he has so fully given himself. His knowledge of medicine has been a great help to him, and he has done much to remove prejudice through a judicious use of the healing art.

When he was in America, in 1871, he met a young man at the Gettysburg Seminary whom it took little persuasion to enlist in our India Mission work,

THE REV. JOHN H. HARPSTER, D. D.,

whose early life was spent in Centre county, Pa., where he was born April 27, 1844. After the ordinary education of his native country-side, and the more important and distinguished training during the Civil War, in which he rose to the rank of captain, he entered the Missionary Institute at Selinsgrove, and subsequently graduated in theology at Gettysburg Seminary with the class of '71. Ordained by the Maryland Synod, December 20, 1871, and appointed by the Board of Foreign

Missions at the same time, in company with Dr. Unangst, he sailed for India, January, 1872, and after a

REV. J. H. HARPSTER, D. D.

visit through Europe, Egypt and the Holy Land, made possible by the kindness of friends, arrived at Guntur,

April 1, 1872. With Unangst, he at once made an extended tour through the field. After acquiring a working knowledge of the language, he saw the vast field and great work to be done in the Palnad, and assumed charge there of a district which through lack of men had been without the direct superintendence of a missionary for over ten years. Making his home at Dachepalli, fifty-six miles from Guntur, he lived in the midst of his people, and verily tried to build up a church, by God's help, in the wilderness. During his period of service of four years, he saw the baptized members increase from 1906 to 3593, and of these accessions over 1300 were in the Palnad field. But his general health failed him, and it soon became manifest that he must seek a change in a cooler climate. Leave was granted him, and on March 22, 1876, he left Guntur, proceeding to America via Japan in the hope that in two years he might again take up his work. But it was not to be so. Years passed. He entered the home pastorate, building a church at Hays City, Kans., serving the Lutheran Church at Trenton, N. J., and for nine years pastor of the church at Canton, Ohio. At the last place he built a large church and gathered around him a loving, loyal congregation. But here again his India work was pressed home upon him, and having accepted an appointment under the Board, in May he resigned his charge and sailed for India, accompanied by his wife, October 21, 1893, over 21 years after he first set out, and 17 years after he had left the work. He is now in the field and has taken charge of the Satenapalli Taluk.

When on furlough in 1871, Dr. Unangst met at Wittenberg College a young man whose life was to be devoted to our Indian work, and who was to take a prominent place in its development in all its departments,

THE REV. L. L. UHL., PH. D.

Born at Millersburg, Ohio, educated at Wittenberg College and Seminary in the days of Dr. Sprecher, ordained in 1872, he left his native land, accompanied by his wife, December 7, 1872, and arrived at Guntur, March 26, 1873. We have already observed how, through want of money and missionary control, our English school was closed and our educational work greatly hindered. It was here especially that the new missionary took hold of the work, and with that earnestness and patience of which he is master, he re-opened the Anglo-vernacular School closed in 1866, set about the development of our whole education service along those lines which have been mainly followed to the present time. He took a deep interest in all educational work. Schools for boys and girls—English and Vernacular Schools—all claimed his attention. During his first term of service he was permitted to see all departments of our educational work definitely organized, and schools of all grades placed on a firm footing.

No small part of his time was spent in the training and education of our future workers. The boarding boys' establishment was under his control, and the attempt to train young men for work whose early educa-

REV. L. L. UHL, PH. D.

MRS. L. L. UHL.

tion had been meagre, received a fair and earnest trial at his hands.

Proceeding on furlough in 1885, after a service of almost twelve years, he was largely instrumental, during his furlough in America, in collecting the money for the new college building—the Arthur G. Watts Memorial—securing over $18,000 for that work. While at home, he carried out the plan of his early years, and took a course in Oriental languages and philosophy at the Johns Hopkins University, Baltimore, receiving the Doctorate of Philosophy in 1889.

Leaving his family in America, he returned to India the second time, sailing November 27, 1889, accompanied by Mr. and Mrs. Aberly and Miss Sadtler, arriving in Guntur, January 18, 1890. Since then, he has done an excellent work, and one which required much tact and patience, in building up the work disorganized by the long estrangements of the congregations in Bapatla and Repalli Taluks, and has out of much disorder brought order and harmony, and out of disloyalty and faithlessness to the Lutheran Church has developed loyalty and fidelity to their foster mother.

The first children's missionary sent out and supported by the Sunday-schools of the Church was

THE REV. A. D. ROWE,

born in Clinton county, Pennsylvania, September 29, 1848. Educated at the country school, he early evinced a great fondness for books, preferring them to all other

REV. A. D. ROWE.

MRS. A. D. ROWE.

companions. Even while at work he had his books by his side, and whenever opportunity presented he was found reading. Spending his winters from the early age of seventeen in teaching school in his native county, he pursued his studies at the county Normal Schools in the summers, and subsequently at Kutztown and Millersville, graduating from both. After his graduation, he was appointed Superintendent of Public Schools for Clinton County at the early age of 22. In 1870 he began to study law at Lock Haven. He connected himself with the Lutheran Church during the ministry of the Rev. W. L. Heisler, pastor of the Jersey Shore Charge (1867), and after determining to study law, he came under the influence of Revs. Diven and Goodlin, who presented the claims of the gospel ministry for his consideration with such effect that in 1871 he entered the Theological Seminary at Gettysburg. Here he met the Rev. J. H. Harpster, who left for India in the winter of 1871, but as yet he had no idea of spending his life among the Gentiles. How his call came to enter the Foreign Field it is hard to say, but at the farewell meeting to Rev. Uhl, at Harrisburg in 1872, December 5th, he came to a final decision. But this he had said: "If God wants me to be a Foreign Missionary, I have no doubt He will make it plain in His own time and way." The spirit which speaks in these words is not apt to be disobedient to God's voice, and though a Board may tell him of its empty treasury, and other obstacles may be presented to his going, still nothing can keep such a soul from his fixed purpose, for he will find a way or make one.

His mind once made up, he conceived the idea of raising the needed funds from the children of the Church, with whom he was a great favorite. In January, 1873, he held the first meeting in St. James' Church, Gettysburg. By March of the same year, the ideas of the missionary were focalized by the Rev. Dr. Barclay of Baltimore, by suggesting a permanent organization, with the consent of the Board, to meet not only his present expenses, but to support his future work. As a result, the Children's Foreign Missionary Society was formed, which contributed largely to the success of the cause of Foreign Missions for many years.

He had expected to leave for India in the latter part of 1873, but so much work was to be done at home, that wisely the Board determined to detain him for a year. During this time he organized three hundred and fifteen societies, with a membership of 21,136, and collected $5,800 for the cause.

He was licensed by the West Pennsylvania Synod in 1873, ordained by the officers of the same body August 19, 1874, in St. Paul's Church, York, Pa., Rev. J. A. Brown, D. D., his honored teacher, preaching the ordination sermon. On the same date, in connection with this service, a farewell meeting was held, at which Dr. Barclay, President of the Children's Missionary Society, delivered an address. A few days later, September the 12th, the missionary sailed from Philadelphia. Taking the overland route via Brindisi and Bombay, he arrived in Madras in November, and in Guntur, December 11, 1874.

Arrived in India, the new missionary found a strange environment. But his energy, nothing daunted by the Hindu's slowness and the enervating climate, soon revealed the strength of the new comer. He said to Rev. Harpster, "I am here to help," and he soon showed a willingness and earnestness that bore out his statement. The first year he spent in the study of the vernacular, and in the work of the high school. He was then put in charge of the Repalli and Bapatla Taluks, and during the terrible famine of 1876-77, he managed with great success the funds of the "Mansion House Relief," and won for himself the commendation of Mr. Digby, the superintendent of the fund in Madras, for his plans and efforts. As he kept the Church well informed by his newsy letters in the papers, and through his books, he maintained that interest he had awakened among the children of the Church.

His plans to establish a large training school for young and promising men who had not received much preliminary instruction were never fully realized. Perhaps had he lived he might have so modified the plan as to ensure its success, but after some years of trial it was abandoned and, instead, the education of youths was urged as the best plan to train workers. It may be well to state, that it seemed to have been no part of his plan to train *paid* workers (into which his plan eventually drifted through the rapid growth of our work, and the scarcity of men to carry it on); but he designed his training school on the plan of a large family, in which he hoped to develop spiritual rather than intellectual powers, and from which he intended to return the men to take a leading part in the work of the village congregations, after two or three years' training. His plans never fully commended themselves to his fellow-missionaries.

But all admit his burning interest in the development of the native church, and as his plans for her elevation show, he had her best interests at heart in all he said and did.

Speaking to Dr. Stork, while on furlough in 1880, he expressed his love for his people, as he called them, and longed to be back again among them. But in many ways he was poorly adapted to work among such a people. His restless, active spirit could not brook their Hindu slowness. He tried his western rush and push in India, and that he did not break down sooner is the only wonder.

Constantly laying new plans, he was all energy in trying to realize them. All this with the climate, which must be reckoned with in India, soon told on his not too vigorous body. He frequently complained of a dull heavy sensation along the base of his brain, and it was soon evident that a change would be necessary, which was hastened by the ill health of Mrs. Rowe. Leaving India April 16th, he reached Philadelphia,

June 13, 1880, and having settled his family at York, Pa., he was soon visiting churches and synods all over the Church with great success. In fact, his duties at home were too great for one who had returned to improve his health. But his zeal knew no bounds, and only at the earnest solicitation of the Board, he took a short season of rest before he returned to India in 1881.

A farewell meeting was held in Lancaster, Pa. September 24th he sailed from New York. Taking the overland route via Trieste, he reached Guntur, November 23d, and was soon busily engaged at his work, and, in addition, undertook the erection of two new bungalows in Guntur. In June, 1882, he moved into his new house, and he said he thought he could *rest* for a time. But rest eternal came to his active soul in the midst of his labors. Stricken down by typhoid fever, it soon was evident that he was in a poor condition to withstand this terrible disease. He took his bed August 12th, and though he seemed to get over the critical days of the disease, he took a relapse, due it is thought to an attempt to work at some matters connected with the Mission while yet abed, and on September 16, 1882, he was called home. He did much in his short service for the foreign cause, both at home and in India. If it be true that "he lives most who thinks most, feels the noblest, acts the best," then Missionary Rowe had service without an equal.

He was singularly adapted by his characteristics to work among children, yet he also was endowed with traits which marked him as an able worker among men. While perhaps no special claims of profound scholarship can be set up for him, yet in executive ability, in energy and clear insight for carrying out matured plans, in a noble ambition to excel for Christ's sake, in an unselfishness for the good of others, in a faith which never lost hope, and in a remarkable cheerfulness amid discouragements and trials, he had few equals. To see a thing that ought to be done was enough. He drove straight for the object, and lost no time in weighing consequences when once he was convinced that the thing was right. It seems a pity that he did not save himself more, but here too he followed Him who "saved not Himself." He had one serious defect as a missionary—one which is mentioned not to find fault with his truly grand life and noble character, but to be a warning to others who may be called upon to take up Mission work in India—he was impatient of delay, he was unable to bear with India's slowness, he wanted to carry all along on the high tide of his energy. Said one of the native pastors who had accompanied him on his last tour, "he was always in a hurry (of course what a genuine native would call 'hurry,' an American would think slow), and he did not take proper care of himself while touring. I wanted him to stop the last noon oñt and rest for a few hours before he went to Guntur from camp. But he would not. Under a boiling Indian sun he struck camp at midday and rode through to Guntur." It was too much for his nervous frame. While building the houses referred

REV. A. D. ROWE'S MONUMENT, GUNTUR.

to above, he went into the sun, when, as the same native pastor said, "it was too hot for me." He must urge on the work. But he has passed into the great beyond to his reward. We would have been much enriched, as a Mission, had he remained with us. But God, in His infinite wisdom, saw fit to take him in the midst of his days of usefulness, and in the full vigor of his noble manhood. We can only close up the ranks and press on, encouraged by his noble life, perhaps warned by his too consuming zeal and activity; and filled with that sublime faith, hope and cheerfulness of which he was so conspicuous an example, in the name of the God of Missions, help to crown his Lord and Master, and ours, King over this dark and caste-ridden land.

The foreign staff was not increased for over six years, not till

THE REV. CHAS. SCHNURE,

educated at Wittenberg College and Seminary, received his appointment. Accompanied by his wife and Miss Kate Boggs, he arrived in India, February 15, 1881. Both ladies suffered greatly from the climate. Mrs. Schnure was so extremely affected and her nerves so much unstrung, that he was compelled to take her to the hills for a change. He had charge of the evangelistic work after the death of Rowe, in September, 1882, till the arrival of Dr. Unangst in 1883. His term of service under the Board was terminated, April 1, 1885, owing to his unwillingness to abide by the Board's decision in regard to existing troubles.

REV. & MRS. CHARLES SCHNURE AND MISS KATE BOGGS.

He died in Philadelphia, 1891, of typhoid fever. He was a quiet and unassuming man, kind and obliging, and had not circumstances been so untoward, he would have made a very useful missionary. The history of the troubles is too recent to write anything concerning them at this time, it can only be said that he allowed himself to be too easily led by others, and lacked independence of character. Yet even here, we cannot say how much circumstances over which he had no control influenced him. He set out with a definite theory, to prove which wrought his own undoing, yet in this he may have been less to blame than others. Personally, except when called upon to differ in regard to Mission matters, we always found him an agreeable companion. He rests, after a life of toil, in peace, and his cause is with the Judge of all the earth, who will do right.

THE REV. L. B. WOLF.

Born at Abbottstown, Pa., November 29, 1857, educated at Gettysburg High School, College and Seminary, licensed by the West Pennsylvania Synod at Littlestown, 1882, on the day that the news of Rowe's death was received; ordained by a special call of the Ministerium, August 5, 1883, in St. James Church, Gettysburg, the Rev. D. J. Hauer, D. D., the missionary's former pastor, preaching the ordination sermon; was appointed to the foreign field in December, 1882, and sailed from Philadelphia, August 25, 1883, for India, accompanied by his wife, to whom he was married July 3d. He arrived in Madras, October 14th, and in Guntur, November 29th of the same year. He took charge of

MRS. L. B. WOLF.

the high school and English work from the principal, the Rev. L. L. Uhl, in January, 1885, and had charge also of the boarding boys' establishment and Guntur congregation till 1890. During his principalship the high school was raised to a college (first in arts), and affiliated to the Madras University, to which the principal was appointed a Fellow by Lord Wenlock, the chancellor of the university, in March, 1893. He is still at work in the college, having been absent for six months recently to take his family to America.

THE REV. W. P. SWARTZ,

educated at Gettysburg, joined the Mission in 1885, and was sent out under the auspices of the General Synod South. He had spent some time, during 1884, in working up an interest among the southern churches, and there was every indication that his work would result in a union of the northern and southern General Synods in the great cause of Missions, and thus lead to a more lasting and permanent union perhaps of the churches, which ought not ecclesiastically be separated. But he had scarcely begun his work, with promise of success, when he withdrew from the field, and shortly after from the Lutheran Church, and thus, after spending a little more than a year in the foreign service, severed his connection with the Mission, which also ended unity of action in Mission work between the two synods. His withdrawal was at a most inopportune time, when the Mission was in special need of his services, when Nichols had fallen at his post, and when the field was left entirely undermanned; and yet, though the cloud was heavy which hung over our work then, God has been pleased to bring us out of this darkness, for the work, so much injured by his withdrawal, has since been largely recovered.

THE REV. JOHN NICHOLS,

born near Shrewsbury, Pa., October 31, 1857, educated in the common schools of his township, in Millersville State Normal School and at Gettysburg, taking a partial course in science in the college, and a regular course in the seminary, was appointed missionary by the Board, April 20, 1885.

He, with his wife, sailed for India, November 21, 1885, and reached Guntur January 30, 1886. His study of the language was thorough, and his progress encouraging. His tastes were scholarly; his aims high. His sermons showed a high order of thought and painstaking preparation. He was inclined, if anything, too much toward the scholar, and may have lacked consequently the practical turn so much needed in the missionary; but he was making all preparation to take charge of the Narasarowpet field, when his summons came to go up higher, and God took him from labor here to triumph above.

After a tour to the Palnad to record for and report to conference the evidence in a serious charge against one of our native workers there, he returned to Guntur, but did not seem at all well, complaining of extreme languor and prostration, both mental and physical. At best never a very strong man, he could not throw off

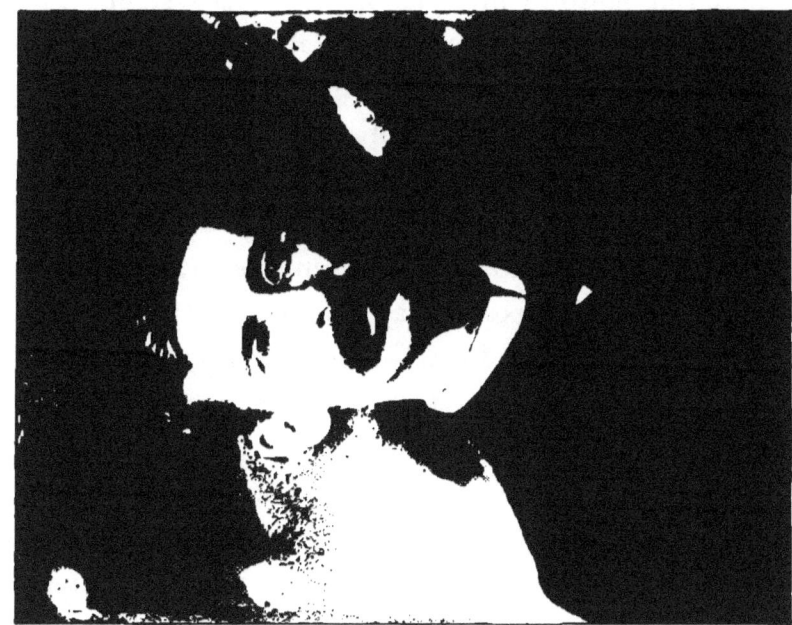

REV. JOHN NICHOLS.

MRS. JOHN NICHOLS.

the malarial poison which had entered his system. He gradually grew worse through the latter part of November, and although he was appointed to preach on the 4th of December, and had prepared a sermon on "The Possibilities of an Immortal Soul," when Sunday came he could not fill the appointment. It was soon manifest that he had typhoid fever. On the 14th day after taking his bed he passed away, surrounded by the missionaries and mourned by all—less than a year after his arrival in the field. God called the soldier, whose weapons were all ready for the warfare. Those that remained had only to say, "Thy will, not mine, be done." The young men of the Church have erected a Mission house at Narasarowpet, the station to which the new missionary was designated, and the "Nichols Memorial" will ever remind the native church of one who gave his life for India's elevation.

THE REV. JOHN ABERLY,

born September 18, 1867, in Carbon Co., Pa., received his academic education at Fairview, and his collegiate at Gettysburg, carrying off the first honors of his class in 1888. After a year at the Theological Seminary he offered himself for the foreign service, was appointed, May 31, 1889, and, accompanied by his wife, sailed for India, November 27th, reaching Guntur via Bombay, January 18, 1890. After two years spent in the study of the language, during which he also assisted in the Bible classes in the college, he was ordained, December

REV. JOHN ABERLY.

13, 1891, by the India Conference, and appointed to the Narasarowpet field. He had charge of this work for two years. He was subsequently appointed by the Con-

MRS. JOHN ABERLY.

ference to take charge of the Boarding School and the

Theological Training School in 1894, and since then has been engaged in the educational department of our Mission. He is also pastor of the Guntur congregation. His work in the Theological School is one of the most

REV. GEO ALBRECHT, PH. D.

important agencies in our native church, the development of which in knowledge and power will largely depend upon the character of the young men who go forth from this Training School.

THE REV. GEO. ALBRECHT, PH. D.,

born in Germany at Gaudersheim, May 4, 1862, studied in the Universities of Berlin, Leipzig, Gottingen and Rotslock, from the last of which he took his Ph. D. For one year he was pastor at Luthe, in Hanover, and for several months pastor of a Mission church in the city of Baltimore. He received his appointment from the Board, April 28, 1892, was ordained, August 7th, and sailed for India via Germany, August 10th, arriving in Guntur, November 24, 1892. His progress in the acquisition of the language has been rapid. He has been associated with Dr. Unangst in the Palnad field, of which he will assume entire charge shortly. He has shown ability in the conduct of his work thus far, and gives excellent promise of a useful missionary career.

THE REV. N. E. YEISER,

born in Adams Co., Pa., was educated at Gettysburg, Pa., in College and Seminary. He was appointed by the Board, April 28, 1892, after two years study in the Seminary, and ordained by the Hartwick Synod, September 4th. He sailed for India accompanied by his wife, October 15th, and arrived at Guntur, December 20, 1892. He is designated *The Young People's Missionary,* by whom he is supported, and has made consider-

MRS. N. E. YEISER.

REV. N. E. YEISER.

able progress in Telugu. He is associated with Rev. Dr. Uhl in work for the present, and has taken up his residence at Narasarowpet in the "Nichols Memorial." He will eventually be in charge of our work in the Vinakonda and Narasarowpet Taluks, and also of the new field recently opened up in Kanigiri Taluk, Nellore District.

The wives of the missionaries and the ladies who have come out under the Woman's Home and Foreign Missionary Society, have not been forgotten by any means in these biographical sketches. It not infrequently happens that the wife of the missionary is as much (if not more) a missionary as the missionary himself. The wives of our missionaries, when their family cares permitted, and even at times to the neglect of what some would consider their domestic duties, assisted in the great work in ways too numerous to mention. Mrs. Gunn, the first missionary wife, carried on schools from the beginning of her residence, and after the death of her husband took up work under the Executive Committee, and carried on her schools and other work with great energy and success—*the first lady missionary from our Church who gave her whole time to the work.* Mrs. Cutter opened the first school for girls in Rajahmundry. Mrs. Unangst took a deep interest in the Christian women and school girls during her many years in India, and with a gentleness so characteristic and Christ-like, won all hearts to her, and commended the Gospel both by word and deed. Mrs. Uhl was largely instrumental in opening the schools for non-Christian children in Guntur, and worked with great energy. Mrs. Rowe interested herself in the girls' boarding school and other schools in Guntur. All did much to strengthen the work of their husbands. Mrs. Wolf had entire charge of Miss Dryden's schools during 1891, and Mrs. Aberly had charge of the girls' boarding school in 1894 while Miss Sadtler was on leave.

However, up to 1884, the work of the women of our Mission was not separately organized, but was carried on as part of the general work. The idea of sending out lady missionaries for special work among India's women, had, however, long before this time been mooted. In the Board's report in 1871 occurs the significant sentence, "The agency of female missionaries (of course other than missionaries' wives is meant) has proved very successful, especially in India; avenues of usefulness have been opened to them that could not be reached by men. * * * We need not only devoted men, but also godly women, to carry forward our various enterprises. The Board asks instructions as to what course to pursue on this point." The instructions of the Synod were, "That the Board * * send forth females as missionaries when proper persons shall offer themselves." Yet eight years later the Board, notwithstanding the previous action of the General Synod, asked that body to endorse its action, not to send female missionaries to the foreign field at this time, as the "time has not come when it would be either wise or expedient to take the step." The Synod approved of the Board's recommendation, and deferred "for the present the employment of unmarried female missionaries in the foreign field." But such is the force of a movement that has once been started that, in 1881, the same body which resolved that the "time had not yet come," rejoiced in the fact that the first unmarried female missionary had actually been appointed, and was in the field!

MISS KATE BOGGS, B. S.,

the first unmarried lady missionary, was born at Zanesville, Ohio, May 4, 1854. She pursued her studies in the Muskingum College to the Junior year, and was subsequently graduated from the Shephardson College at Granville, with the degree of B. S., in 1878. For two years she taught school at Dickson, Tenn. Appointed by the Executive Committee of the Woman's Home and Foreign Missionary Society, she sailed for India, November 27, 1880, arriving at Guntur February 15, 1881. But no sooner had she arrived than she was prostrated by the climate, from which she has never fully recovered. Her only Mission in India was to *suffer* for the cause to which she has given herself. After all medical aid proved unavailing at Guntur, she tried the effects of a cooler climate at Bangalore, but this too failed. She was compelled to leave India, and arrived in America, April 15, 1883. She has in good measure been restored to health, and was happily married to

MISS KATE BOGGS.

Rev. J. F. Shaffer, D. D., of Delaware, Ohio, July 3, 1884. Her zeal and interest are unabated in the great work in which she was pioneer, and her earnestness is shown in all work of women for women, whether at home or abroad.

MISS ANNA SARAH KUGLER, M. D.,

fourth daughter of the Hon. Chas. Kugler, was born at Ardmore, Pa., April 19, 1856. She graduated at the Woman's Medical College of Pennsylvania in Philadelphia, in the class of 1879, and was for three years engaged at the Norristown State Asylum for the Insane, as assistant resident physician. She offered herself to the Woman's Home and Foreign Missionary Society to come out and start medical work among women, but received little encouragement, and it was only when she was willing to subordinate her medical ideas of missionary work that she was at length sent. Appointed by the Executive Committee and confirmed by the Board, June, 1883, on August 25, 1883, she sailed from Philadelphia and arrived in Madras, October 14th. Delayed by floods up country, she did not reach Guntur till November 29, 1883.

The idea of a Medical Mission, though not fully adopted by the Home Committee, was soon pressed upon her attention by the wide field open to such endeavors, and it was only a matter of a few months' observation till its real usefulness and efficiency as a missionary agency were fully demonstrated. Yet, even then, it was a hard task to start such work against preconceived notions, in certain quarters, as to its real position as an evangelistic agency.

Her first furlough to America was in 1889. Leaving Guntur, January 13th, she was at home till the middle of 1891, doing good service while there in stirring up a

MISS ANNA S. KUGLER, M. D.

more intelligent spirit and interest in this great cause. She was present at the conventions of the Woman's Home and Foreign Missionary Society in 1889 and 1891, and returned to India October 10, 1891. She opened a new dispensary for women and children, February 15, 1892, and is now having under course of erection a hospital. In 1893 she was asked to speak at the Chicago "World's Fair" on Luther Day, and was temporarily absent from the field from July 28th to January 25th, to fulfil this engagement. Already her expectations of the medical work are being in a large measure fulfilled, and, when the new hospital is ready for occupancy, the work will be placed on such a footing as to ensure its enlarged usefulness among those agencies which shall be most effective in moving India for Christ.

MISS F. M. DRYDEN, B. A.,

born April 13, 1862, educated at Carthage College graduating with the class of 1883, offered herself for foreign service early in 1883, and was appointed in April of the same year. Leaving Philadelphia, August 25th, she reached Guntur, November 29, 1883. Her work has been chiefly in connection with organization of schools of the Zenana Mission. Her activity in this department has won for her the approbation of the English government, and her Industrial School for Muhammadan women and children has attracted much attention, and its exhibition at the "World's Fair" was most creditable and won a medal. In 1888, her health failing, she took a short furlough to Australia, and was absent from the field about four months. In 1891 she was on seven months' furlough to America, and returned, October 10, 1891. She has completed about ten years' ser-

MISS FANNIE M. DRYDEN, B. A.

vice, and has been instrumental in the organization of a large and growing work.

MISS SUSAN R. KISTLER

was born in Perry Co., Pa., October 25, 1863. She was educated at Bloomfield Academy and also attended

MISS SUSAN R. KISTLER.

Hartwick Seminary and St. José. She offered herself for the Indian work, and was appointed in 1888. Leaving America, October 13th, accompanied by missionaries of the American Board, she reached the foreign field, December 1, 1888. Her work has been at Narasarowpet

MISS AMY L. SADTLER.

and adjoining districts, both in school and Zenana departments. She has permanently made her residence in

Narasarowpet, where the Executive Committee has built a substantial Mission house. She is still in the work.

MISS AMY L. SADTLER,

born in the city of Baltimore, educated at Lutherville Female Seminary, offered her services and was appointed in 1889. Leaving America, November 27th, she arrived at Guntur, January 18, 1890. Her work has been in connection with girls' boarding schools and in the Zenanas of Guntur. Owing to ill health she left Guntur, on furlough, February 24, 1894. She expects to continue in her work, and hopes to return soon.* Her service has been four years.

All told, our foreign staff is small. It has had many vicissitudes; death and ill health have thinned its ranks; it has passed through severe trials; but God has ever watched over His workmen and guided them in their work, and though often discouraged, they have gone on in His name and under His banner. May He keep all faithful to their high trust!

* In 1896, Miss Sadtler became the wife of Rev. Geo. Albrecht, Ph. D., and is now with him in the Mission field.

CHAPTER VI.

INDIAN STAFF.

Early Efforts, Gradual Efficiency, Present Conditions, Future Prospects.

IT is axiomatic, that to bring India to the acknowledgment of Christ Jesus the sons of the soil must be enlisted. To accomplish a task of such stupenduous magnitude, with such inherent difficulties of language and climate, natural character and religious faith, it is of the first importance that men trained on the field—men of the people—filled with their own peculiar ideas, but filled too with the knowledge of Christ Jesus and led by the Holy Ghost, must be raised up to carry forward the vast undertaking.

The land "to be possessed" is great. The languages are many. The climate is hostile to the foreigner, and makes all effort exhausting. The foreign missionary has much to learn before he is in a position to be really effective. However, the Foreign Staff is most important, in view of all the facts which missionary history has developed. It is essential to the successful carrying on of the work. This is admitted by the native workers themselves. A consecrated Foreign Staff, experienced in the organization of mission work and educated in all the institutions of the Hindus, must, for many years yet, control the vast undertaking. Undoubtedly, though the number and efficiency of the native workers are growing year by year most encouragingly, yet the necessity of supervision and help in life and faith, and in the evolution of a native church among this varied Hindu community, become only the more imperative as one more fully understands the real situation. The Foreign Staff can do no greater work than to direct ably and successfully the native in its work. And it is evident that such work requires men of the first order of mental and spiritual endowment, real leaders among men, full of faith and the Holy Ghost, on fire for the cause of truth, and yet not so full of enthusiasm as to have no place for discretion, tact, and all the lower orders of endowments, which tell so much in the guiding and direction of men. It matters very little what view a few of our native leaders may entertain in regard to this position or office of the foreign missionary, for it is manifest that it is the one in need of which our little nascent congregations stand, until a more liberally-educated native staff of workers can be put into the service, and the congregations can look after themselves and cease to require either the advice or assistance of a foreign Church. If a foreign missionary grasps the situation clearly and studies to learn what the office of overseer or bishop really must be in such a land, he will then be in a position to do the greatest good to the largest number—to let his light shine all around him.

But we must face matters as they are, not talk so much of what they ought to be. For the present, then, while it is most important to the work of the Church that native pastors, teachers and evangelists should be chosen (we make no attempt to classify, and would prefer the term native workers, always using "*native*" in a good and honorable sense), and sent into the great field, yet it is of supreme importance, when the characters of these native workers in the majority of cases are remembered, and especially their education and Christian experience, their late coming out of heathenism, that strong and faithful bishops, in whose veins the Christian life of centuries runs and whose disciplined minds are the product of the Christian life and culture of the ages, should have the guidance and moulding of the Church. The financial connection with the Home Church, while an important consideration, is by no means so vital as to require this supervision. But it has its bearing on the whole question of Foreign Superintendence.

But, while thoughtful men see all this, still the great question of India's evangelization must be answered through a consecrated and devoted body of native workers, filled with the spirit of the Master, in His name preaching the truth and making disciples of the nations. How such a body should be chosen and set to work becomes a question of the deepest moment. The Church must raise up, under the guidance of the Holy Spirit, the laborers for the great harvest field. The work of the infant Church, not to speak of the large outlying non-Christian mass as yet unreached by the gospel, calls for men of a variety of talents, gifts and graces; and that Mission is most fully alive to its responsibility here, which can lay hands on the native workers best fitted for each duty in this complex task.

Reliance on the Holy Ghost is needed, and the prayers of the Church should ever ascend, that men may be rightly guided in making this choice.

What the relationship should be between the native and foreign worker cannot be definitely answered, as in such a question the character, standing and attainments of the native as compared with the foreign worker must be fully considered. Nothing, however, can be a greater hindrance to the work of the Church than the usurpation of too much authority on the part of the foreign and too little regard on the part of the native worker for his foreign helper in the Lord. In general, mutual confidence and support should exist between them. The authority of the Church must be exercised with an even-handed justice; and when the native workers have shown themselves fully alive to this rule and have, by their acts in subordinate spheres, shown themselves worthy, there should be no hesitancy to admit them to equal rights and privileges in managing all ecclesiastical affairs. But, whether with this should go equal support from Mission funds has been and will always be a vexed question.

Speaking on native workers, the Rev. Mr. Jones, of Madura, in the Decennial Conference in 1892, said:

"Nothing is more evident than that our ordained native brethren, in common with intelligent and influential laymen, must some time be prepared to enter into the heritage of responsibility and authority, and to hasten the autonomy of the Church in India, *their term of apprenticeship* should begin at once." But the experience of the British government in the matter of self-government should cause us to hasten slowly. This is certainly a safe principle, and one which will work out the best results in church life. To establish the peculiar organization of the Church that carries on the work may not be deemed either wise or necessary, but to adopt a form of Church government that will best suit the conditions of the people and their natural life should be the aim of all who have this work in hand. For the present, to utilize every man in that place in which he can do the most for the cause must be the task of the missionary, and just so far as he succeeds in getting the right man in the right place, so far will he be a really successful bishop in this great field of Christian endeavor.

But we can only touch on these vital questions which the missionary must solve, and on the solution of which depends so much. It is the Native Staff of our own field to which we now turn our attention. Historically, the native worker became a factor as soon as he could be found, without great question at first as to his fitness or abilities. What he could do, in the opinion of the foreign missionary, he was set to do, and his work was not too narrowly examined in this first and infant stage of the work. Among one of the first adults to receive baptism was a man by name *Stephen*, and he was soon set to work to teach a school for boys, while his wife, Rebecca, opened a school for girls in the *palem* or hamlet. The missionary writes: "The experiment is cheap and must be tried, and if God smile upon the attempt it will prosper."

Any employment to which a convert could be put in these early days was deemed worth the trial. Something was regarded better than nothing—a plan which seems to have worked well, and it is enough to say that it is the plan taught by the Parable of the Laborers, where the command: "Go work in my vineyard, and whatsoever is right I will give thee," shows clearly that those who are available were to be employed.

Schools were soon opened to train men for work, but the missionary did not fail to use the men of one talent till others could be got ready. The same is a wise policy now. There are frequent allusions to show how wide-awake the early missionaries were to the training up of a body of workers, whose life and hopes were centered in the land.

In 1854 the Synod took upon it the special training of three young men, and determined a course of study to fit them for the work of the Mission. In 1858 the President of the Synod urged immediate attention to the great and important work of training native workers, and the Synod, in its action, resolved: "That it is its conviction that the preaching of the gospel to the masses must ultimately be done by native agency. We deem it necessary to raise up a native ministry." At this time the number of men under training had increased to five, the Synod's only regret being that funds were not available for increased work along this line. No central school seems to have been opened in those early days, and each missionary seems to have selected and trained a few of the best men he could find at his own station. The financial report of Rev. Heyer for 1853 shows charges on account of boarding students at Gurgal; and it would seem that the Grönnings had both boys and girls under training at their station. In 1854 100 Rs. were sent to Rev. Snyder for girls under training at Guntur, while he (Heyer) used the same amount for boys, in his station at Gurgal. Later on, in 1857, entries show that twenty men and *two women* were employed on salaries, varying from 2-6 Rs. ($1.03), their chief work being in the schools of the Mission at Guntur, in the Palnad, and at Rajahmundry.

This was the beginning, undoubtedly, out of which gradually developed the evangelistic workers, or it may be truer to fact to say, these teachers combined the twofold office of teacher and preacher. In 1859, there is for the first time a statement of the native workers; and the list runs as follows:

Catechists, 2; Colporteurs, 2; English school teachers, 7; Telugu school teachers, 5. This was the force at work after a period of 17 years. Not all were Christians, but the majority were. But from this time forward the native staff began to grow, both numerically and in efficiency. It may be well to show this growth since 1860. The following table will show what changes have been wrought as the decades have passed by. It must be remembered that the efficiency cannot be tabulated. It should also be remarked that not all the teachers in the English school are Christian.

	Native pastors.	Sub-pastors.	Catechists.	Sub-catechists or Village preachers.	Helpers.	School Teachers.	Evangelists and Colporteurs.	Bible women.
1860	..	..	2	..	..	12	2	..
1870	..	..	2	..	..	29	41	..
1880	2	..	4	42	..	49	41	..
1890	2	5	19	100	48	232	4	7

It may be well in this connection to say a word about the functions of these workers. All along our history the highest place had been assigned to the unordained catechist, until within recent years there was established another grade of workers, between the catechist and the native pastor, viz.: the evangelist, lately called sub-pastor. All our workers beneath the pastor's grade are *unordained*, and have only the office of teachers and preachers. They are entirely under the supervision of the missionary, and must report monthly all the acts of their ministry.

172   AFTER FIFTY YEARS.

The Sub-Pastor, as both his name and rank imply, is a candidate for the pastorate. The catechist is the most honored and trusted assistant of the missionary

SONS OF SUB-PASTOR N. ROBERT.

in the work of the congregations. He is his helper in all the complex management of the church, and is a general superintendent under the missionary. The sub-catechists are all candidates for the catechist grade, though as a matter of fact many of them are neither fitted for it by education or character, and never will reach it. Below these are the helpers. These men are sent to new congregations to hold the faithful together, to assist the catechists in their work, and in general to do whatever work the missionary sees ought to be done, and for which no trained worker is available. Their educational qualifications are not very large, but they are generally chosen for their influence in the congregation as Bible readers. This class of workers is only temporary, until better men, more highly educated and experienced, can be furnished. The school teachers, with the exception of some in the college, are all Christians. Their work is to train the children of the congregations in both secular and religious knowledge. They are truly teacher-evangelists, when they rightly fulfil their office; and their work in the Bible and catechism is quite as much a part of their daily task as the ordinary secular subjects. Many of them are the wives of our catechists and sub-catechists. Our work as a Mission began in the school and it has continued to prosper along these lines. It has insisted on the training and education of the young, and its growth has proved the wisdom of this plan. The British government assists these little schools, according to rules laid down in its Grant-in-Aid code. It does not interfere in the least in the religious instruction imparted; and the grant drawn is both an incentive to the teacher, as the mission allows him half, or all of it, as a supplement to his salary, and also a help to the Mission in extending this work among the people. As a rule no school is opened in a village until there is the beginning of a Christian community; but it may be said that this rule has been made as much because the funds for the work are limited as because it is deemed a wise plan of work. Such a rule did not obtain at first, when all were heathen and the school was deemed the best place to inculcate the truths of the gospel.

The rapid growth of our staff may be noted. In 1870, though two stations, Rajahmundry and Samulcotta, had withdrawn, we had over twice as many teachers as in the four stations in 1860. While in 1890 the whole number of workers in the Mission had risen to 417, as over against 36 in 1870.

But not only in point of numbers has there been an increase, but what is better still, there has been a growth in intelligence, efficiency, in a clearer apprehension of Christian truth and in character and life; though much remains to be desired in all these particulars yet, and character and teaching must be blended more and more into life before the gospel has gained its highest triumphs.

But why, undoubtedly it will be asked, has there been such a slow growth in the pastorate, or in the ranks of ordained workers? This question is a delicate one, though, undoubtedly, one which is most natural. It is not so easy to answer. To say that we as missionaries have found it a wise policy may be quite satisfactory to us and to those other missionaries who agree with us in this policy, but it will hardly satisfy those who want to see a self-supporting and independent Church in India in this generation. It may as well be admitted that we, without in the least limiting God's power, do not much believe in such an ideal and near future. It is a safe principle, we believe, that the native pastorate should be developed in accordance with the needs and wants of the native Church.

Had we twenty native pastors we could not employ them in the best way, unless we had twenty charges over which to give them pastoral oversight. And then the question of support would arise, and our people are too poor to support them. Even should a number of contiguous villages be united in one charge, the matter would be by no means settled. The missionary could not at this stage withdraw from the work and hand it over to the native pastor. This we say with all due respect to our native brother. We cannot as yet see that the highest welfare of the Church would thus be subserved, although we are shaping our plans and looking toward the time when such charges will be formed, and when either the whole or part of the pastor's support will be furnished by the people themselves. But we move in this matter only as we can see the possibility of success, and so long as things are as they are we cannot agree that the native church is in a position to stand unaided without foreign money or missionary supervision. The Church cannot in our opinion dispense with the foreign missionary's influence, even had it ample means, (which it has not,) to support its own pastors under such an arrangement as the one above indicated.

Then too, delicate as is the point it must be touched. In this whole matter the character of the men whom you want to put into the ranks of the pastorate becomes your first consideration. The majority of those prepared for such work come from the ranks of that part of the nation whose past is one of slavery and oppression. The idea of self-government is foreign, and it is sure that nothing is so apt to turn a man's head and make him dizzy as the sudden elevation to power. Were we to follow in the wake of a sister Mission, remembering all the supposed questions of advantage involved, we could ordain *twenty-five* men to-morrow, but we very much fear we would repent the step before the year would be out. We must have men educated in a higher school than the college, and teach them things which can only be learned by experience and time, before we lay hands on them in holy ordination. We must have tried and tested men to shepherd the little flocks; and the latter must be trained to meet and assume the ideas of self-government before we can safely entrust them with their own affairs or send them shepherds. Undoubtedly it would be much easier to turn them adrift to get along as best they could, than to continue to superintend and guide their ways; but it would not be best. And this we say, even though we open ourselves to the charge that we will never teach them to walk unless we cease holding them. We are quite ready to raise up for the pastorate any and all whom we find worthy, but not until we are persuaded that the churches have reached at least such a development in self-support as to co-operate with the pastor and undertake his support. Even then, such are the difficulties of self-government and the development of a true Church-life among this people, that we would still contend that all should be left *tentative*, and the missionary should have perfect right to step in and interfere in the management of the congregations. It is quite evident he would be needed on many an occasion when the right conduct of affairs would demand his presence and help. Of one fact we are quite satisfied, that we are not ready to hand over the managing of the Mission under its present organization to *superintending native pastors*. We shall endeavor to do our best to set apart a true pastorate on the following lines as soon as we see the times are ripe for it: A few contiguous congregations, which can afford to pay some part of the salary of a pastor, will be organized into a charge and a worthy man placed over them, to whom the Mission will give the entire management of affairs, subject, however, to the final approval of the Mission in all serious matters. He will be sent on trial, and a careful watch will be set over his work all the while, it being an established principle that so long as a part of the support of the pastor comes from the Mission treasury, he must be amenable to the Mission. As time passes the work will become more and more independent of missionary help and supervision, and the missionary will have time to devote to other fields of labor. Roughly such has been the plan which has been contemplated, but we hasten slowly in all these matters, and trust no development which does not seem to insure a strong discipline and an intimate association in all that relates to these little congregations. Our native staff grows apace now. We must see to it that it is not only a growth in numbers, but in zeal and earnestness as well. We must not rest content with present attainments, but by every means in our power enhance its efficiency and faithfulness, its character and devotion. By a system of examinations, no man can rise until he satisfies the Mission of his mental fitness. Until he is 40 years old, he must yearly attend these examinations in such subjects as will fit him for his work. Nor will passing these examinations entitle him to promotion into a higher grade. He must show himself an approved workman, and his Christian character must be such as to elicit the confidence of the missionary as well as the people among whom he has labored. Those whose educational qualifications fit them for higher positions are advanced as wisdom deems best, but no man is thrust into a Christian worker's post until he has been on trial in that work which is required of him, it matters not what his educational qualifications may be. Character and experience are more important than intellectual education in the development of mission work. But it is true that men, who have been educated in our High School, quickly step into the first rank if their heart is in the work; but they must begin below and show themselves approved workmen before they can enter higher positions for which their education fits them.

Thus an additional burden is laid on the missionary, but one which he does well to take up in thorough earnestness, to superintend and direct a course of reading and study for the men under him. It is a duty of the first importance, and one which under the divine blessing will in the end bring the richest harvest. Thus will be discovered the men on whom he can depend, and those best suited for the various duties and positions of his work.

Too great emphasis cannot be laid on the necessity of highly educated workers for some branches of Mission service.

The requirements of the pastorate will largely depend upon and be shaped by the work to be done. But in actual contact with heathenism, no weapon which education and grace can furnish is unnecessary, and the keener the intellectual weapons of the man, provided always he be under the divine guidance and does not simply use them for his own glory, the better will he do the work of an evangelist. Right in this connection we would like to say, that in every Mission staff the times seem ripe for the organization of an arm of service which aims chiefly at the evangelization of the non-Christian community, and for which work special training is necessary. And this we say, not that we think that every missionary and native worker should not use every opportunity to do the work of an evangelist, but because we believe special talents are required and special experience needed for such work—such in fact as will only be discovered by actual work. What we mean is, that when a worker's *forte* seems to be that of a preacher to the non-Christian masses, he should be set apart for that work by his Mission, whether he be European or native. We pass on now to a consideration of the Mission's organization.

CHAPTER VII.

ORGANIZATION.

Division of the Field and Work, Character of the Work undertaken by each, Medical, Zenana.

How a work is done depends largely on its organization. Organization is by no means everything, but it is a great deal in the accomplishment of great undertakings.

Ten men organized, each set at his own task and doing it with his might, can accomplish more than twenty, when each imagines that every other man's work is his, and that he must try to do all. This is evident.

The best work some men do in Missions is to marshal the forces and drill the recruits, lay down lines of work, and make rules for the general and combined onward march against the foe. That Mission which has a definite work for every man and woman in it (supposing always they rely on God and go forward in His name), will accomplish the best and most lasting work. By no means is it enough to *set* men at a post of duty; it is quite as important to *set bounds and fix limits* and *conditions*, make rules and regulations, and circumscribe the work required so as not to interfere and produce dis-

ZENANA HOME, GUNTUR.

order, but so as to secure that harmonious development which is ever the result of a combination of parts under a general plan and central control. Much time is wasted and great confusion is sure to result where there is no definite line of march for each one, but where each one is trying, irrespective of his neighbor, to reach an end which though good in itself has no reference to him who labors next him. It is *when a Mission moves as one man* that there is power; just as the unity of faith elevates, quickens and sends on the souls of thousands rejoicing, so does unity of plan and definiteness of aim inspire men and women united in Christian work. All God's works are done in perfect order.

Our Mission organized itself into a Conference as soon as there were two or three to confer. It is true it is difficult for a few to come to conclusions when differences arise; but still conference, though it may fail to conclude, results in great good in the way of mutual interchange of opinion. The organization among the missionaries as time went on extended to the field. It was districted and assigned to different missionaries. In course of time, though much later, different men were set apart for special work. Those stations were fixed at first by which centers of operation were secured. At these centers all the work along the various lines was more or less organized and pushed forward. Schools were opened and outdoor preaching from village to village commenced by the missionary and his helpers, until gradually a system of work was established, of which the missionary was the centre. The great weakness of a system like this, is that a man must be what no man is, a universal genius—one who can do anything and everything he undertakes equally well. The missionary tries to carry on the complex work of the Mission, and finds his efforts so divided and his energies so taxed that he can push nothing vigorously. Is it possible for a man to be doctor, preacher, school-manager, builder, and a dozen other things at once? Can he do justice to any of them? Division of labor must tend to efficiency in missionary work as well as elsewhere.

Our present plan is to have central educational work for the training of Christian workers in Guntur, to which all the pupils must come. A central boarding-school for such training relieves the district missionary from such supervision, and he has his time for work among his congregations and their schools, and for preaching to the unevangelized masses. In dividing the field into districts, we have followed the divisions of the government, noted in a previous chapter. At present there are five divisions, formed as follows:

1. Bapatla and Repalli Taluks; 2. Guntur Taluk; 3. Sattenapalli Taluk; 4. Palnad Taluk; 5. Narasarowpet, Verinkonda and Kanagiri Taluks. This division is not very equal, either as to size or importance, but with more men at our disposal the work can be more evenly divided.

In Guntur itself there is a missionary in charge of

the Telugu congregation and Boys' Boarding Establishment, and another has the College and the Printing Office under his management.

The missionaries of the Woman's Home and Foreign Missionary Society are separately organized under Zenana (Home Visitation and Education) Medical and Educational departments, and they have also made some attempt at a division in the field, so as not to cross each other's paths in work.

It is unfortunate that this division of labor has been

MUHAMMADAN WOMEN AT WORK IN INDUSTRIAL SCHOOL.

made the occasion of considerable criticism, both within and outside Mission circles. This criticism is the result of a misunderstanding of the functions of each department of work.

Men and women are spoken of as Evangelistic, Medical, Educational and Industrial missionaries, and these names are used, as certainly they should not be, to discredit or enhance the evangelistic character of the work of some over others. It is certain that the end in view of all work, it matters not what name it bears, is the evangelizing of the people, and these titles are only indicative of the organized plans by which in missionary circles it has been deemed wise to carry on the great work. Experience has been the guide in these plans or modes of work, and should certainly have much to do in determining the question as to their continuance; more in fact than the cry of outside critics, who, though ever so well-meaning, know little of, and often care less for, the work of missions.

In our Mission, the evangelistic missionary has the village congregations and the direct preaching of the gospel to them and their heathen neighbors committed to his charge. But any one who knows anything of this work knows that he must spend hours and days in doing that which cannot fall, by ever so great a stretch of the term, under the head *evangelistic.*

The Educational missionary must of necessity spend considerable time in the routine of teaching, other than biblical subjects; but this, by no manner of means, excludes him from the work of the evangelist, or gospel missionary. His school or schools become his church, in which the Word of Truth is daily taught and enforced. Especially does the missionary, who is set for the training of young men for gospel work in the Mission, occupy a position of peculiar advantage in influencing and guiding those to whom the Mission shall look for future workers.

A DISTRICT BULLOCK COACH.

The Medical missionary who dispenses medicines for the healing of the body has an opportunity of organizing evangelistic effort among the patients, which can only be understood by those who understand India's social and religious system. And so let not the contention of any who would emphasize these terms beyond their missionary sense, deter friends in their support of any part of Mission work on the ground that it is not evangelistic. Every department is intended to bring the gospel to bear upon the minds and hearts of the people, and the wisdom of such organization has been abundantly proved by experience. Missionary history is its defense.

With these preliminary remarks let us examine the development of the different departments of our Mission: 1. THE MEDICAL; 2. THE ZENANA; 3. THE EDUCATIONAL; 4. THE EVANGELISTIC. It is not claimed that this is an exact division of the work; as has been hinted above, the divisions often pass into each other. But under one or the other of these heads it is possible to group and explain every branch of the work, without doing violence to our logical sense.

In point of time the medical work of the Mission was the last organized, but it was by no means neglected even before there was any regular organized effort. The first missionary, "Father Heyer," took a course in medicine, as he saw what opportunities such a work would present to his hands for reaching the natives of all classes. When in America in 1846–7, he for some time studied medicine, and as the rules of the profession were rather lax then, he soon got the diploma of a practitioner, and on his return made great use of his acquired knowledge, especially in the Palnad work, which lay far away from any government dispensary where the people could get medical aid. Later on fever remedies and cholera mixtures were used by all missionaries with excellent effect, and simple diseases whose character can soon be mastered, and which can be easily relieved by the use of simple remedies, were treated with great success, enlarging the sphere of the missionaries' influence. So important were these deemed that they were published in a little work in Telugu for the help of all who could read, and especially for the use of our native workers, who were thus enabled to render immense assistance to the poor people among whom they labored. The Rev. Dr. E. Unangst has during the long years of his Indian career, though not a regular practitioner, made great use of the healing art to reach the different classes, and his treatment of the common diseases of the country has been so successful as to ensure him great popularity in the District. For years he has carried with him quite a supply of medicines, and also has been granted the assistance of a native compounder, to put up and dispense under his directions among the people such medicines as he carries.

The medicine chest is a valuable ally in all missionary work throughout the villages, and all our missionaries have made more or less use of it. Their medical work, however, was rather a subordinate part of their service. The missionary did not push it; it was rather forced upon him by the circumstances of the people, yet all realized that it was a most effective agency to gain the confidence and good will of the people.

Up to this time the work was mainly confined to the villages, among the poorer classes of both sexes. But the necessity of such work has been to a large extent

removed through the active and humane measures of
the Government in establishing Dispensaries in all

A GROUP OF MISSIONARIES.

parts of the country at such distances as to make them accessible to large numbers. In each Taluk medicines are dispensed at one or more places to out-patients, and arrangements made for the reception of a few in-patients. But these Dispensaries are all in the hands of *men*, and Hindu custom makes it an almost impossible thing for the better class of females to be benefited by these institutions. That woman was born to suffer, has been so fully accepted by Hindu philosophers that they have grown indifferent to much that she must endure, which is due not so much to necessity as to the dictates of hoary custom. But philanthropy got a glimpse of this misery of Hindu women, and Missionary Societies, touched by the woe and misery which must result from a lack of medical help, and impelled by the great Healer, who ministered to the body as well as the soul, soon set apart for this special work *ladies*, whom Western advanced thought and life had been preparing. Such work has only been made possible by the views entertained in the Western world in regard to *woman's work*.

As already stated, it was some time before the Society felt that the time was ripe to send out a medical missionary, even when the lady was ready to come. But it was not long after, under rather unfavorable circumstances, the medical work was begun. The one who started this branch of work, as we have elsewhere noted, was Miss Anna S. Kugler, M. D., but she was not engaged to come out as a *medical* missionary; the times were not deemed ripe for such a departure, and so it happened that she was almost two years in India, as a missionary, before her time was entirely devoted to this branch of work and she was set apart to organize, what all must admit who know anything about India, was from the moment of her arrival a most pressing and

GRINDING CHUNAM (PLASTER) FOR THE NEW HOSPITAL.

urgent need. She, however, during these years did not cease to utilize her professional abilities in many ways, and in a quiet way demonstrated the fact to all that such a work was urgently demanded and would prove the very means needed to help in other fields of work, and in itself be a powerful evangelizing agency. All objections entertained by the authorities at home vanished before the plain facts of actual experience, and in the *latter part of 1886* the medical work of the Mission was started, and a dispensary for out-patients opened in the town of Guntur. During 1887 the work grew rapidly, the number of patients treated being 1,353. In 1888 several new dispensaries in different parts of Guntur were opened, with a view to popularizing the

THE MISSION DISPENSARY, GUNTUR, WITH MISS DR. KUGLER AND BANDY.

work among all classes, and one was started at Mangalagiri, a town thirteen miles distant from Guntur, which proved a valuable means of gaining access to the people, and awakening confidence in the missionary, especially among the female population—the part of India least accessible to gospel influence.

The plan of work is very simple in these dispensaries. Their evangelizing character is ever kept prominent. While the women and children wait, there is a Bible woman at work reading and teaching, sowing the seeds of the kingdom. The lady doctor goes in and out among the patients, dropping a word here and using an opportunity there, and the good work goes on. With the

WOMAN'S HOSPITAL, GUNTUR, (JUNE, 1895).

medicines for the healing of the body, the higher and more blessed, for the soul, is sent into the homes which had never even heard the news of the Great Physician before. One must remember the condition of things in India to appreciate what the real position of the work of healing, thus carried on, is in the bringing of the gospel to the women of the land.

But more than this has been done. Steps were taken in 1885 looking toward a hospital for the treatment of in-patients, and several thousand Rupees were subscribed by the missionaries of the Mission in India. With this beginning the work has taken hold of the women of the church and fifteen thousand dollars have been raised for these new buildings. The work of erecting them has been taken up and will be completed within a year. The first of these buildings, the dispensary for out-patients, was opened in February, 1893. A bungalow for the resident doctor is also in course of erection, and when all is completed, there will be a plant worth about sixty thousand Rupees ($30,000.00). Toward this expenditure we have succeeded in getting a grant from the different Local Fund Boards of the District, and it may be that from all Boards sixteen thousand Rupees may be realized, at least a partial promise to that effect has been made by the District Board. The plan of the hospital is for thirty beds, but the maternity ward cannot at present be erected, and must occupy part of the main building. Should the District Board make good its promise, we may at once proceed with this ward also, but even without it we shall be in a position to carry on our medical work in a very satisfactory manner.

It is hoped (though hopes are not history) that the hospital may be endowed by and by. A start has been made, and three beds have been endowed, by the subscription of one thousand dollars each.

But this work is just fairly started. Its history must be made, and then written. We are sanguine that the future will fully justify all our hopes for this branch of Mission service. Its popularity is secured already. Its influence is being felt; its power for good has been seen; its hold over the women of all classes is vast, and its quiet moulding effect on the Hindu life at its most vital point is beyond estimate.

ZENANA WORK

is the attempt to reach Hindu women of the better classes in their homes, by sending teachers to them. The Zenana of India is an institution not of Hindu origin, but introduced by the Persian conquerors of the land in the dim past, and is an institution belonging to the Muhammedans. It means the part of the house occupied by the women. This custom of the seclusion of females has grown into a very exacting one. To keep married women of the better classes in zenana or purdah, that is, concealed from the view of others than their husbands and near male relatives, has all the binding force of religious law among the Hindus.

It became early evident to those conversant with Hindu customs and anxious to reach all classes, that if the message of Christ was to reach these shut-up women, thousands of the great Hindu and Muhammedan races, it must be taken to them by *women*. It is no part of our task to show how this idea was gradually forced upon the Christian consciousness, but it has not

ZENANA LADIES AND BIBLE WOMEN.

been many years since the first lady missionary was sent out to find her work within the closed doors of the zenana.

And what a struggle it has been to gain entrance, even for gentle woman! She alone held the key to open the closed doors, and she alone, after many bitter struggles and disappointments, has opened the door, and is opening it to thousands of India's homes. Here is a mission for consecrated women, beside which the efforts of the knights who tried to wrest the Holy Sepulchre from the infidel's hands bears no comparison, for the holy shrine of the home must be rescued from superstitious and heathen rites, before the true light of Christ can shine into India's heart. The effort to take the homes of India for Christ has been fairly joined. The battle here, as in the nation, will be long and hard. The work of thousands of consecrated women will be needed. The end may be far down the future, but it will surely be *light in darkness.*

The effort to reach the Hindu of all classes, to be successful, must lay hold upon the home and the home life, as a most important factor in India's regeneration. If the home is changed, the root of the matter has been touched. The Hindu is strong in his household gods, and naturally women, being more religious than men, cling to them with a tenacity of which men know little and very often care less. Organized effort among those classes which are allowed out-doors becomes an easier, though not a less important task, than the work among those whom custom keeps behind the purdah. But the significance of the work among the secluded women belonging to the wealthier and higher classes cannot be too much emphasized. As a rule, their husbands are the leaders of the Hindu and Muhammedan community, and more or less, have themselves enjoyed a western education and understand something of our western modes of thought and life. They feel that their wives are much inferior to them in point of education, and attribute it to their customs.

Impelled by a desire to do these secluded women good, and teach them the new life of their western sisters, the Christian women of the world organized societies to carry on this work which they plainly saw must be done by *them, if it is to be done at all.* But the beginnings were hard. Hindu and Muhammedan closed doors were not easily opened, even to the gentle knock of western sisters. Many were the bitter disappointments which had to be bravely faced before the doors flew open, and a welcome hand in pleasant *Salaam* was raised. But the initial difficulties, though by no means all overcome as yet, are gradually growing less formidable, and through the medical and school work, the women have been made to feel that the missionary lady is their best friend, and may be trusted with the most secret doings of their home life.

With us as a Mission, hardly more than fifteen years have passed since the attempt was made to teach in the Hindu homes. Speaking of the effort to educate the children of the better classes, the Report of 1875 says: "Then (when education has done its work and prepared the way) the doors of the Zenanas will not be shut so closely." Up to this date practically nothing had been done in this branch of work, and not until 1878 was any formal work undertaken by the Mission. It is true, that before this the missionary ladies visited the school children in their homes and encouraged the Hindu ladies to visit them in return, and any results, however insignificant at such a period, secured in this unorganized way, cannot be judged by their apparent smallness, but must be weighed by the real hindrances which must be removed before such a work can fairly be started.

Through the aid of Mrs. Pardhasarathy, a native Christian lady, educated in the Free Church Mission School, Madras, who has done much to develop woman's work among her non-Christian sisters of Guntur, Mrs Uhl, in the year 1878, began a systematic visitation, and through Mrs. Pardhasarathy gave regular instruction in a few homes of some of the leading native gentlemen. This was a small beginning, but was the seed-corn of the Zenana work of our Mission. It was soon found that a special agency was needed, and in 1880 the Mission made a call for one or two unmarried missionary ladies for this and other work among women. We have seen how that call was answered. After the organization of the Zenana Conference, an organization of wives of the missionaries and the unmarried missionary ladies sent out by the Executive Committee, this department of work was not neglected, and in 1885 the Report shows that considerable progress had been made, that Hindu and Muhammedan homes were being regularly visited, and that some of the barriers to the work were being gradually removed. It was made manifest that the work begun in our girls' schools among the better classes, must be followed up if the best results were to be attained. The girls were taken from the schools at such an early age, owing to the peculiar custom of Hindu early marriage — child-marriage — that, when a fair start had been made and the most encouraging results were about to be expected, suddenly custom interposed and the girls were removed from schools by their relatives or husbands, and all progress stopped. Here was place for more thorough organization of the Zenana work. In 1889, classes were opened in the homes by which the work begun in school was carried forward in the home, and these classes were placed under rules similar to the schools, the Government being willing to give grant-in-aid to this work.

The Bible work was not disturbed by this arrangement, and the importance of regularity in work was emphasized by the yearly inspection of the Government Inspectress, and by the regular examinations. The homes have been entered and the work commenced. A wide field of usefulness presents itself and workers are needed here, both native and European. Progress has been made, and by no means the least, is that into many homes our native Christian women are admitted, where 18 years ago hardly a European lady could gain access. The work must be pushed along these lines of organized effort; and the harvest will be gathered here as elsewhere in due season, if we faint not. The organization of such work has also been effected at Mangalagiri, Bapatla and Narasarowpet, and is limited only by the lack of suitable workers and supervision.

CHAPTER VIII.

ORGANIZATION CONTINUED.—EDUCATIONAL.

General Considerations—Its Place in Missions—Duff's Early Work—Schools in Relation to Government—The Position of Higher Education—Girls' Schools: Early Origin, Present Condition—Mixed or Congregational Schools, Their Work—Boarding Schools, Their Necessity and Aim—High School and College—Mission Colleges, Their Aim—The Development of our College, Its Position in our Work.

THE school has played a prominent part in India's evangelization from the first among Protestant Missions. Even among the Roman Catholic Missions of late it has taken a new start, as their large College at Trichinopoly testifies, the second largest in South India. But we should limit the term school by *Christian*. The Christian School, in which Christ is honored and His truth taught, was early conceived as a wise method of reaching the people of the land. It is doubtless well known that in the beginning it was the only agency employed by which the better classes could at all be reached. Of more recent years some doubts have been awakened in the minds of some missionaries and others, as to its real position and efficacy as an evangelizing agency.

REV. L. B. WOLF, A. M., PRINCIPAL OF WATTS' MEMORIAL COLLEGE, AND TEACHERS.

Questions have been raised as to the place that *higher education* should have in a legitimate missionary propagandism, and the opinions of missionaries in some quarters have been somewhat divided as to what amount of money should be in justice spent, and time given, to the education of those who are not Christians —Hindus and Muhammedans and others—in Christian schools, presided over by Christian Missions and supported in part by Mission funds. It is a question which in some quarters has been so mixed up with local coloring and prejudice, that it becomes difficult to separate the personal element from the main issue. It is best to take this method of missionary work, and examine it in those particulars in which all agree that it is without doubt a most legitimate method of evangelization.

All agree that *primary* schools among the lower classes, from which the largest accessions to Christianity have come, should be maintained, at all cost, for all who wish to come, whether heathen or Christian; but they should be made parochial, *i. e.*, instrumental in the dissemination of Christian truth as well as secular knowledge. High schools and colleges should be maintained, all agree, for the education of Christian youths for superior service in the great and growing field of Christian endeavor. Then, too, there is practical agreement that schools *for girls* of the higher classes of Indian society may, with perfect justice and consistency, be regarded a legitimate missionary undertaking. So far there is agreement. Now the question arises, to what extent should schools and colleges be used as a proper missionary means to educate those who are non-Christian in the higher branches of Western thought, supposing always that Christian men, so far as possible, are the teachers and professors in such schools, and that the Bible is made a regular part of the course of study? As Dr. Hooper said at Bombay in 1892: "This is the *burning question* in some quarters." To answer it fully is no part of our task, yet a few words may be said, which it is hoped may prove helpful to those who want to examine the question at greater length.

From the time of Dr. Duff, of the Scottish Mission of Calcutta and subsequently of the Free Church Mission, the Christian school and college have taken their places in the rank of missionary agencies, though it must be confessed, not without some struggle. For more than twenty years the disadvantages were more largely those which must ever be experienced in a land with the prejudice and hatred of change which are found in India. Hindu opposition was fierce and was especially directed against the school and college, as these were the most directly antagonistic in showing to the young of the nation the unscientific and false knowledge of the Hindu religion. Then came the government schools and colleges, supported by the government with great liberality from public funds, neutral in matters of faith and religion, having all the influence of position and money at their back—they seemed to threaten the very life of the Mission school. Certainly, if education can be had and Hindu faith left untouched, all will go where such conditions are found. But victory for the struggling Mission's schools was near at hand. Even this formidable rival could not crush that which had been successful. The Indian government awoke to the greatness of the task to be done, and determined to enlist in its work of education outside bodies, which were allowed, under rules framed by the government, to work in this great field. The famous dispatch of 1854, the Magna Charta of the Indian nation, in matters pertaining to education, settled once for all the battle between those who fought for *Oriental* as over against *Occidental* culture. English won the day, and with this victory all schools and colleges began to take rank with those of the government. The idea of imparting European knowledge through the media of the classical languages of the East was abandoned; the dream of the orientalists was not realized. It was determined not only to utilize *English* as the medium, but also to encourage schools and colleges, other than government, to accomplish the great task of the enlightenment of this vast empire. By a judicious system of Grant-in-Aid, all societies carrying on schools and colleges could reap the benefit of substantial support from the public funds, and in the course of time it contemplated leaving the entire educational work in the hands of outside parties.

This was the opportunity for missionary bodies to establish their schools and colleges, and as wise men they have availed themselves of this grand opening, and are now so much to the front, that after 40 years all the Government schools and colleges, except in the Presidency towns and a few elsewhere, have been closed or handed over to private management, and the only rival in the field is the *native school* and *college*, which must work under the Dispatch of 1854 on the same conditions as the Mission school.

Briefly this represents the historical genesis of missionary higher education. Each step was a struggle. Now let us turn to the examination of the classes which these schools reach. Admittedly, they were looked upon by the Government as calculated to give an English or Western education to the better classes of Hindus and Muhammedans. Here Government was compelled to stop. With the religious instruction in these schools it could have nothing to do in view of the well defined neutrality-policy in matters religious to which it was committed. But missionary bodies seized this as the very means which God had providentially placed in their hands, to evangelize the rising generations of the better classes, and to bring the power of the gospel to bear upon the very centre of Hindu civilization. And the condition of the nation was such as to justify them in their efforts. The gospel had to be taught and enforced before the nation would heed. The large bulk of the nation had not heard the gospel, nor had it any special willingness to be brought under its influence. The Christian school, however, furnished the ground on which to meet and inform the rising and most hopeful portion of the nation, the young men, who were to lead India in the near future. If Christian Missions had not taken their stand, and embraced these providential opportunities to instil Christian thought and life, it is certain they would have failed to appreciate the great work to be done. Granted that the field among the lower classes is so great that it cannot be properly cultivated with the present resources at hand, yet it remains a fact, that unless our schools for the better classes had been maintained, the most influential class of the community would never have come under gospel influence. With our colleges and schools for non-Christian lads, thousands are still strangers to the influence of Christianity, because they will not attend our Christian schools, but prefer to go to those influenced by Hindu religious thought and life. If it were not for Mission schools for professedly non-Christian lads at the present day, all the higher education in India would be in the neutral hands of Government, with no religious instruction, or in the hands of those hostile to Christianity, and bent on a purely Hindu propagandism. As it is, no legislation in regard to religious instruction can be enacted. Attempts have been made to introduce "conscience clauses" in some of the "Grant-in-aid" codes, but they have not amounted to much and have been more honored in the breach than in the observance.

But those who have had some doubts in the legitimacy of this missionary propagandism have been urged to this by the paucity of the results, which made its continuance a question. To men who enter into mathematical theories of mission work, such an objection has great weight; but surely when we take the task the Church has set for herself in India, we cannot measure influence by such a commercial standard or give up work at the dictates of mathematics. As Dr. Miller so wisely said in London, in 1888, at the great missionary conference: "If the western thought now flowing into Hinduism could bear with it the influences of Christianity, the mighty mass might be awakened into new moral and spiritual life." From such an intermingling of spiritual power with western thought the benefit must follow slowly and surely, as in all great movements. He continues: "Let the historic truth be taught about the plan of love that was gradually unrolled, till it was summed up in the *life of lives*, and by the aid of the Spirit it would bring hearts and consciences to the point of view from which the value of a Saviour is understood and felt." It being clear that God has an open door into Hinduism through the school, no one should be deterred from entering it by the cry of the smallness of the immediate results. The great Hindu society, by means of these schools, is being leavened by the gospel, and its very unity has helped to hasten this end. Hardly an educated man can be found who has not imbibed, with greater or less clearness, a considerable body of Christian truth, and can speak with more or less accuracy of God's great plan of love in Christ Jesus. However he may be affected by it, it is clear that to impart Christian truth is the aim and highest duty of all missionary bodies, and since the school furnishes a splendid arena for this, the reason for its existence is justified. It should be remarked that though this agency is a considerable drain on the Mission treasury, a considerable proportion, and sometimes a large one, is met by the fees of the students and the Grant-in-Aid of the government, which will depend on the number of students and the efficiency of the teaching staff.

With these general remarks we pass to the account of the school work carried on in our Mission. As the Lutheran Church had its origin in the great intellectual awakening of the 16th century in a university, it is only following out her history that she should lay considerable stress on this method of evangelization. For the sake of clearness, it will be helpful to divide the work. We shall consider it under (1) Girls' Schools; (2) Mixed or Congregational Schools; (3) Boarding Schools; (4) English or Anglo-Vernacular Schools and the High School and College.

1. GIRLS' SCHOOLS. Our Girls' Schools are sometimes designated Caste schools, *i. e.*, schools to which only the children of the better classes go, or rather which have been established for the special benefit of those classes, in order to gain among them a way for imparting religious truth. India must be viewed from the standpoint of its social laws, institutions and customs, to see

the importance and need of such schools. We must reach the home. The mothers and sisters must be influenced by the leaven of Christian thought and life; and the opening into caste-ridden India, with its closed doors for the Christ-child, has been through the school. It is here that a start was made among the better classes of women, and it was begun before either medicine had

GIRLS' BOARDING SCHOOL, GUNTUR.

been utilized or the zenana teacher had entered the tightly-closed doors of Hindu and Muhammedan homes. Against this work for women the most sturdy opposition has, from the first, been waged, nor has the conflict by any means ceased. The Hindu could see no special reason for educating his daughters. This was the first barrier that had to be broken down. He could see benefit in educating his sons. It gave them a market value in the community, and procured for them service under the government. But why he should spend money on the education of his daughters or send them to school, was something for which he could see no good reason. First, then, the persistent opposition to educating girls at all had to be met and overcome. At present this outer wall has been more or less successfully scaled. The workmen are face to face with their great task to *educate not only mentally but morally and spiritually.* To this work the customs of the country present almost insuperable difficulties. Just when a girl is about fairly started, her parents, or more likely her husband, object to her going to school on the ground of her advanced age, and stops further progress. But eventually this objection must yield, especially if female teachers can be secured, to obtain whom all possible efforts are being made.

The religious opposition is not more open here than elsewhere. It is persistent everywhere, and it may at any time break out at the most unexpected place. At present it has assumed the form of an effort to start counter schools under Hindu management. "We must have our own schools," they say, "to educate our daughters, just as we have them for our sons." But as yet little has been done in these schools. The community are not keen enough on the question of the education of girls to throw themselves into this work with any great earnestness. But we must expect opposition, and from this quarter stirred up by religious opposition it will most certainly come sooner or later. Missions are not secure by any means in any work which directly attacks the central Hindu unit. The first attempted organization of a girls' school is referred to by the Rev. Gunn in his diary, and was started in 1848 in Guntur. It must have been opened some time before this in 1846–47; among others than those of outcaste

HINDU GIRLS' SCHOOL, CHILAKALURUPET.

origin who attended there were twelve Sudras (fourth Hindu caste) and one Muhammedan girl. An attempt at that early date was made to educate the girls in *English*. But limited funds and strenuous opposition to such an innovation made it slow work. Allusion is also made to a girls' school organized by Mrs. Cutter at Rajahmundry, and carried forward through the kind

MISS MINNIE MOSES, WITH NORMAL CLASS OF 1894.

help of English friends for several years from 1853-5; but nothing is said as to what classes of the community attended the school. It is pretty certain that no girls' school had been opened which was attended by all classes of the Hindu community in our Mission before 1875. In March of that year a school for girls was opened, not under Mission control, but with the support

SAMALADAS AGRAHARAM.—GIRLS' SCHOOL.

and patronage of the missionaries and English residents of Guntur. Mrs. Rowe visited this school frequently. In 1876 the Mission authorized the opening of two Girls' Schools for caste children, and in February and March ('76), they were opened, and for the first quarter had (the one in Samaladas Agraharam) 23 and (the one in old Guntur) 24 pupils. Our work among these classes is less than twenty years old. But the work has both multiplied in numbers and grown in strength, as the following will abundantly show:

Year.	No. of Schools.	No. of Pupils.	Brahmins.	Vysyas.	Sudras.	Muhammedans.	Others.
1876	3	47					
1880	3	137	34		59	11	35
1891	17	735	146	109	344	98	38

But figures can only represent in a feeble manner the vast advance made in this work. It was customary, at first, to pay all children who attended the school, sometimes money and later a native jacket and an occasional cloth. Now all this has been greatly changed, and in the main only scholarships, and annual prizes for attendance and general scholarship, are awarded. But more than this has been gained, and that a slight appreciation for the education of women is being felt is shown by the fact that Rs. 191, according to the report of 1891, were contributed by the Hindu community toward the support of the schools. To any one who knows the sturdy opposition to these schools from the first, and anything of the Hindu nation and its lethargy, this is most encouraging, nay, almost phenomenal. The cost of the schools has always been borne by the Mission, assisted by generous Grants-in-aid from the

Government Educational Department, which has ever been keenly alive to this work, on its secular side at least, and is only too happy to assist missionary agency to the extent of available funds. In 1891 the grants received from the government amounted to one-third the cost of maintenance. But though these schools are a heavy drain on Mission funds, they are justified in the eyes of every missionary who has given the work of evangelizing India a moment's thought, and especially to any one who has examined the difficult question of teaching the women of the nation.

The organization of these schools under the Zenana Conference has not stopped in Guntur, but under Miss Dryden's management, schools are carried on at Bapatla, Perala, Cherala, Amaravati, Mangalagiri, Ponnur and Chebrole, and under Miss Kistler, at Narasarowpet, Chilakalurpet, Rompicherla, Vinukonda, and Dachepalli. In 1893 there were 1175 pupils in school, 19 schools organized and working. In 1875, in the language of the report, this school work was begun among the better classes with the greatest *caution*, children were given presents of money and clothes to attend, and little or no attempt was made to interest the children in scriptural truths for fear of breaking up the schools; while, at the present time, the people of the same classes ask us to give them schools in large outlying villages, and offer help toward their maintenance. Undoubtedly this work can now be pushed to a much greater extent; is only in fact limited by the means at hand for efficiently managing it and imparting religious instruction, and with the latter carried on in a systematic manner, is quietly becoming a mighty factor in training out the *old* and bringing in the *new*, opening up a new life to the Hindu female community, and bringing with it the needs of a new freedom. A good start has been made, and workmen tried and true are needed to extend this work and make it more effectual in the dissemination of the blessed gospel of Christ Jesus.

II. THE MIXED OR CONGREGATIONAL SCHOOLS.—As we have already noted, these schools are for the education of the children in our congregations of both sexes, hence called mixed. They are all primary, according to their grade, and have only in a few cases reached the highest class in that grade. The majority of them have only three classes, and impart an elementary education in *Telugu* only. With the grossest ignorance among the lower orders in India, it was an absolute necessity that schools like these should be organized, and they have ever proved the wisdom of that policy which called them into existence. Of late years the social condition of the lower strata of population has been engaging the serious attention of the government. Their ignorance, helplessness, poverty, the oppression of the superior orders under which they live, the cruel customs of the past which make them little better than slaves, have all been forced upon the attention of the government. Even in the British parliament their hard lot is being discussed, and measures set on foot to alleviate their condition. All this has brought the missionary considerable encouragement in his hard labors for these people. The schools have gotten the ear of the government, and liberal Grants-in-aid are being made to encourage all Missions to engage in this feature of their work among these poor downtrodden masses, and to aid them in every legitimate way to elevate these, at present styled the *depressed* classes of the Hindu community. It must be remembered that these schools are as a rule among the poorest of the poor—those who have barely enough to eke out a scanty livelihood. Their servitude to the higher orders makes them an easy prey to their former masters, who are yet, in many cases, practically their masters and owners, through debts of long standing from which they are too poor to free themselves, and too ignorant to understand when in the natural course of events they have paid them. But the education already imparted is beginning to change the order of things. The poor dependent is learning that he may be a free man of which he never dreamed before, and with a little caution and independence he may get rid of much of the harshness of servitude. With a growing knowledge the perplexing question, too, of debt contracted with his higher class neighbors is passing away, or at least he is beginning to demand and understand the relation and rights of debtor, and intelligently make arrangements to pay off his indebtedness. It is not hard to see how things must work, when all the power and intelligence are on the side of the creditor. Hence the change effected by these schools in the whole social order, and the great good secured to these poor ignorant classes, serfs of the soil till freed by English rule, are patent.

But as an evangelizing agency these little schools have the first claim on missionary support. Great as is their philanthropic influence, their religious importance in the spiritual elevation of the masses is greater and more important. With this end in view they were opened at the first and are continued at present. We find them our most powerful ally in imparting religious truth. Every teacher is expected in a systematic manner to impart religious truth as the most important part of his daily work, and to enquire how this work is done, is part of the duty of every missionary as he visits the congregations in his towns. Although the principle now followed is not to open a school in a village before Christians are found there, yet such a rule did not exist at first. *The school frequently preceded the church, and out of it the church gradually grew.* The first thing our tried English friend told "Father Heyer" was that he would fit up one of his outbuildings in which a school could be started, and services held. And so it turned out that our Mission, like many others in India, *began in a school.* Stephen, baptized July 4, 1847, was employed as a school teacher in Guntur, and his wife, baptized in September of the same year, opened a school *for girls.* Examining the report of the missionary in 1848, it is pleasing to note that all parts of the educational work now carried on had a fair start, for Rev. Gunn reports a Telugu boys' school in the Mission compound with fifty-two pupils, of whom twenty-five were Sudras, twelve Pariahs, five Muhammadans, six Roman Catholics and four Protestants, and in old Guntur, sixteen boys and twelve girls taught by Stephen and his wife Rebecca; besides these a girls' school and an English (one in which the English language was taught) school having twenty-five pupils, of whom two were Brahmin, seventeen Sudras, two Muhammadans, one Pariah, one native Christian, and two East Indian. The New Testament, Peep of Day and suitable religious tracts were used in imparting religious instruction, a portion of the scripture was memorized. Much hope was entertained for this branch of work. These beginnings were small, and yet they are especially significant as showing in what way this Mission, along with many others, reached the people. The instruction of the youth in Sunday-school was deemed one of the surest ways to reach the Hindu community, the present condition of our schools still emphasizing the wisdom of this plan. Steadily the work has grown, the schools have increased in numbers and efficiency, as better teachers have been trained. Our present plan confines such schools to our Christian communities, but it is not so insisted on but that it would be deemed a wise policy and a proper expenditure of money to plant elementary schools in heathen villages, especially among such classes as have not yet been reached by gospel influence. A plan like this has been often talked of, and the wisdom of beginning schools among the Sudras in the villages, who in many cases are as ignorant as their countrymen among whom our work largely lies, has been admitted, and the plan has been only deferred for lack of funds and trained men to put in charge, so as to carry out the plan successfully. It must come by and by, as we are quite as sure it will open up a way for the gospel among these classes, as our earlier attempts among the lower classes. It may be well to remember that the Sudra community constitutes the backbone of the nation, and a church among them means from the start a self-supporting institution.

The following table shows the growth and development of our elementary schools since 1848:

Year.	No. of Schools.	No. of Pupils.	Christians.	Non-Christians.	Hindus.	Muhammadans.	Others.
1848	3	93	5	88	44	7	37
1858	16	396	*	*	*	*	*
1868	21	211	*	*	*	*	*
1880	49	1079	664	415	*	*	*
1890	196	3263	1654	2021	329	34	1658
1893	{ 19 / 208	1234 / 4000	59 / 2020	1175 / 1980	} 1375	102	3757

A few words of explanation may be needed to understand this table. The column marked "*others*" is in-

* Not determined.

tended to mark the non-caste or lower classes of the community who attend our schools, but are not reckoned as strictly belonging to the Hindu race. It will thus be seen at a glance that non-Christians are brought under religious influence in large numbers, as over half of all the pupils in these schools are non-Christian. We welcome all to our schools. It will be seen that during the last few years the growth of this work has been very rapid. That it was not stronger early in our history was not so much due perhaps to want of opportunities, as the want of means to carry it on. The teachers for our congregational schools are all Christians. Most of them have been trained in our Mission; many of them have been pupils in our boarding schools, and have begun work as teachers as a preliminary step to other and more responsible posts; and their qualifications, while not of as high a grade as is desirable, are yet steadily becoming higher. From these schools we hope to draw our future workers. From them they pass into our boarding schools, and then into our higher schools for training in both general and religious knowledge. As the Christian community grows in intelligence, and in a due appreciation of these schools, our native Church will develop and take a higher place in Christian thought and life. For, while it may be conceded that education does not of necessity develop moral and spiritual life, still, as all must admit, it is a great aid in the acquisition of that knowledge on which faith leans, and becomes a powerful factor in the development of that life which feeds on food divine. No one can fully estimate the real end subserved by these schools in the development of our infant Church.

But we pass on to a special class of schools, which have all along been recognized as a necessity in the present state of Indian Church life.

III. THE BOARDING SCHOOLS.—This name is, no doubt, misleading when considered from an American standpoint. A boarding school generally means one at which boarding is furnished by the authorities of the school and payment made by those who attend, as part of the regular fees levied. The difference in our Mission boarding schools is, that while the first is true, the latter is true only in a very modified sense. As yet only a very small amount of the cost of supporting the students is paid by their parents and friends, the larger burden resting on the Mission. It is not hard to find the reason for this, when the poverty and ignorance of the people are remembered, the former making it impossible for them to pay the whole cost of supporting their children, and the latter making them unwilling to send, much less pay, for their education. So the Mission stands in place of a parent toward the child, and, with the exception of clothes (and in some instances these are in part furnished), the cost of books, food and tuition is borne by the Mission. The real grounds for this are found in the growing demands of our work and the necessity of employing native workers for its effective accomplishment. The wisdom of turning out and putting into the great field as large and as strongly an equipped body of natives of the land as can be raised is so manifest that it need only be mentioned to commend it to all. But in the present condition of affairs we must educate the youths for this work. The Church here has not risen to that state when it will be done without our assistance. It is not a question of our wanting to do it, but one of necessity, if we desire to train a native staff of workers for our growing village work. Two departments have been opened, one for boys and the other for girls, the former under the management and support of the General Conference, the latter controlled by the ladies of the Woman's Home and Foreign Missionary Society and supported by that body.

In order to develop the pupils *out* of their heathen notions and surroundings and give them a fair chance to get new ideas, they are admitted into the schools at an early age, before habits have been formed, the Mission standing toward them "in loco parentis" not only as to their training and support, but also, to a great extent, as to their marriages and future work; their whole lives, in fact, are more or less ordered by the Mission.

In the girls' school all instruction is in Telugu. The standard of the schools compares favorably with a grammar school. It is in the standard of Government, a lower secondary school with a normal department, and a practicing school for the training of teachers.

The boys' school divides itself into two sections. The one embraces those who study English in the Anglo vernacular branch schools of the Mission and in the high school of the college. Their course is limited only by their abilities to cope with the difficulties and by their freedom from early domestic entanglements. The other section comprises those lads whose entire instruction is in Telugu, they being usually retained in the school until they have reached, if not passed, the lower secondary school. They are limited to the vernacular in their studies for several reasons. They have either had no chance to study English in their primary training, or else have begun to read when their age made it very difficult to master English to such an extent as to make it useful in their future work. It must be borne in mind, that a lad who begins English the third year of his schooling must be allowed not less than ten years before his English studies will be of great material benefit to him in his future study. The value of such a course is not by any means forgotten, nor does the Mission regard the time required as too great, but it finds itself greatly hindered by the boys themselves, by their parents who want to contract early marriages for them, and too often by the want of ability and an earnest desire to continue their studies.

Both sections of the boys' school are under religious training, as it has always been the plan of the Mission to develop the two sides of education simultaneously. Those lads who read in the higher classes in the high school, take the regular course of that school. At present only a few have reached the higher classes. Those who study in the lower classes and get no further, whose acquirements are too limited in English to continue their studies in that language, are sent into the Telugu training department for a year or two, before being sent into Mission work as teachers.

It may seem strange, but one of the chief difficulties in this work is to get the boys to continue their studies until they become really well educated in both secular and religious subjects, or until they attain to that standard of training which our college affords. It is saying nothing derogatory to the boys, to say that this difficulty is due to a want of native ability as well as to the lack of the habit of the true student. This must not be wondered at. A race of students, to a large extent, is born, not made. For centuries out of mind those from whom our converts largely come were slaves, mere things in the hands of a superior race, with no intellectual training, no cultivated tastes for learning or books, and no chance to improve themselves. So they find it hard, after such conditions, to make the most of these new opportunities which their emancipation has brought them. It is encouraging, however, to note that this great hindrance is gradually disappearing as the atmosphere changes by which these children are surrounded. It will be a work of time, and one in which much patience must be exercised, before they will be in a position to make the best use of the opportunities, which the Mission so freely secures for them.

Another and most potent hinderance to their higher

training is the system of *early* marriages, which has filtered down from the highest to the lowest of the nation. It is the end to all real training, and higher education and culture, when girls of thirteen and fourteen, and boys of fifteen and sixteen, assume the cares and burdens of a family. This is a *root trouble*, and, with all our influence, it is hard to eradicate it. We must exercise the most unbounded patience, be firm, and calm withal, when the parents of a clever lad begin to urge matrimony just about the time he is really in a position to do his best studying and make most progress, the most beneficial for his future work. Imagine what the American nation would be if marriages were contracted at so early an age, and training and education thereby almost stopped.

We know there are ancient customs which are urged to justify these early marriages, and that the peculiarities of the nation are such as to make them, to a certain extent, seem very plausible, but this does not in the least change our contention that they form one of the most serious hindrances to the training of our young men and women. We must, however, take things not as we would have them, but as they are, and as wise builders make the best we can of our material. Marriage, it has been discovered, can be deferred, and a little pressure is not wrong when wisely applied.

Thus having shown the grounds for the existence of these schools and their relation to our organized village work, as well as a few hindrances to their higher efficiency, we desire to look briefly at their historical development. Suffice it to say, it was among the earliest ideas of our missionaries to open these training schools. In the account of Father Heyer, in 1853, entries are found of expenditures on account of boys and girls' boarding schools, both at Guntur and Gurjal. At this time Rev. Grönning lived in the Palnad and had charge of the work there. In the same year an estimate of Rs. 360 was made for the maintenance of these schools. In 1859 the number under instruction had risen to 16 pupils. The following shows their growth by decades:

	Boys.	Girls.
1859	2	14
1869	2	6
1879	22	16
1889	150	48

During the early years their numbers vary greatly in the decades; however, it is certain that no great forward movement was made in these schools before 1874, and the reason is patent, as we had no missionary staff to look after the field or develop the work, sufficient for the proper carrying forward of different departments of mission endeavor. At the present time it is the determined policy of the Mission to have both schools under the management of a foreign missionary, and to push the work of training men and women with new zeal.

But more encouraging than the numerical increase has been the educational advancement of these boys and girls. Both schools have been most liberally helped by the aid of government grants toward the maintenance of a suitable staff of instructors, and toward the building of a large new dormitory for the girls, one-third of the cost of the latter being given.

A new building is about to be erected by the native church as a memorial to Father Heyer, as well as a mark of our fifty years of labor and progress.

The most important part of the training in these schools is that which arises from the personal contact and influence of the missionary. They have also been excellent places in which the evils of caste can be rooted up, and the most humane and sensible ideas of the gospel can be practically exemplified. There are societies in both, that in the boys being called the "Brothers' Society." It conducts several devotional meetings during each week in the schools, and keeps alive the practical piety of the members. The other in the girls' school is named "The King's Daughters," and is conducted on similar lines to such organizations in America.

We mention here that every effort is being made to get the parents to help bear the cost of their children's education, and a fair and encouraging start has been made, to which we may refer later on in the chapter on self-support.

IV. THE HIGH SCHOOL AND COLLEGE AND ITS ANGLO-VERNACULAR BRANCHES.—The idea of using English as a medium of imparting to the higher classes in India a knowledge of our western science and thought, originated not much over sixty years ago. Only forty years have passed since the war of the Orientalists, *i. e.*, those who wished to employ the classical and vernacular languages as the media of instruction, and the Occidentalists, those who wanted to employ English, has ceased. The great prince, both in education and higher English education as an evangelizing agency, was the sainted Dr. Duff, of Calcutta, who, under the Church of Scotland, began his work in 1830. Nor should we forget the services at the same time of the Serampore missionaries. Soon the Anglo-Vernacular school became a recognized agency in most Missions for reaching the higher classes, whose caste views made it difficult to bring them under the ordinary preaching, but to which this agency appealed with special force.

The government encouraged this from the first, because by it the administration was furnished with men to carry forward its different departments—men trained in English, and conversant in the vernaculars of the many-tongued people over whom their rule extended; while the missionary saw in it the means he must use to bring the gospel to bear on the rising generation of the most influential class of the community.

We have already examined the question at considerable length, at the beginning of this chapter; but a few thoughts in addition may be in place here. In many parts of India the higher classes were not at all reached, except as they were gathered into these schools. This has been true from the beginning of Missions, and is no less so now. It makes no difference, if it can be shown that it is a wilful refusal to hear the gospel, which has been maintained by these higher classes. If it can be shown to be such, the more reason has the missionary had to use any and every legitimate means to break through this determination to have nothing to do with the gospel. And even if it were evident now that the higher classes did not want the gospel, and attended these schools only to get the English education, which would be a passport to future employment under government and elsewhere, Missions would be justified in maintaining these institutions, only making them more evangelistic, as larger numbers of the masters become Christian, and as the Christian student gets a more honored place among the non-Christian.

It was not till 1854 that the great universities of Bombay, Calcutta and Madras were established, whose special object has been to guide and limit the course which western education should take, and test by examinations the results of all schools and colleges affiliated to them. These have in forty years wrought wonders, and the growth of education under these universities has been phenomenal. All the higher ranks of government service, the law, medicine, engineering, are opened only to those who have passed the university tests as a preliminary. The character of the training is constantly being elevated to suit the demand for more highly trained men. It is made impossible by government enactment to bestow a public appointment upon one who does not have the educational qualifications fitting him for such post.

No man who knows India at all can fail to see what a splendid field this offers for the Mission school. Here is a field all ready, and he has only to keep up to the university and government requirements, and no questions will be asked as to his Christian work or instruction among the students. This is secured by the non-interference-policy of the Indian government in matters religious. He can teach and preach his faith six days in the week, and organize a good Sunday-school on the seventh, if he uses the proper tact. To the maintenance of the school the government is willing to assist by a Grant-in-aid from one-fourth to one-fifth the cost of the school. If the missionary does not enter this "open door," he leaves the whole work of the education of the young, who will soon be the leaders of the nation, to the Hindu schools or to government schools, where in the first case there has developed of late years an active anti-Christian propaganda, and in the latter a negative attitude on all questions of religion, though on purely moral issues the government is wide awake. In addition, these schools furnish education to all Christian boys who want to pursue a study of the English language; in fact, they are for all, without regard to race, faith, color or creed, and become the common meeting ground where stubborn race and caste customs and prejudices of centuries are receiving their most deadly blows, and are being gradually undermined.

In the Madras Presidency alone there are 126 schools, recognized by the Director of Public Instruction, in the high school department of which there were 3,431 examined by the University in 1893. These were for boys only. In addition, there were seventeen *high schools for girls*. The whole number of boys and girls reading in the high schools alone of our Presidency in 1894 was 30,666, of whom 28,231 were boys and 2,435 girls. Of these high schools for boys fifty-eight were under Mission control, and of those for girls *all but one*. Of the 143 schools, twelve are under Roman Catholic influence. There are thirty-four second and fifteen first-grade colleges, affiliated to the University of Madras. Of these, eighteen second and six first-grade are under Mission management, of which thirteen second and four first-grade colleges are in Protestant hands. It is a remarkable fact, and one that Protestants do well to remember, that the Roman Catholic Church, whatever her policy has been elsewhere, is pushing her educational work among the higher classes of India with great earnestness.

There are, then, twenty-four Christian colleges, *i. e.*, colleges in which Christian men and women teach, and whose aim is to further Christianity; or almost fifty per cent. of the education in the Madras Presidency is in the hands of the missionary. Out of a total of 3,310 graduates, since the founding of the University forty years ago, 2,283 belong to the Brahmin, 609 non-Brahmin, 30 European, 71 * East Indian, 287 native Chris-

* Mixed parentage.

tian, 28 Muhammedan, and 2 Parsee community. When the numerical strength of the Christian community is considered, the showing of this class is very commendable.

Among these affiliated second-grade colleges our Mission college stands, numerically holding an average place, opened in 1885 and occupying the twenty-first rank in age.

The first work, among the boys of the Krishna District, by means of the Anglo-Vernacular schools, was started about five years after the founding of the Mission. In 1848 there was a school, in which the English language, the Holy Scriptures, Luther's Catechism, the History of England, Geography, Geometry, Grammar and Arithmetic and translation from and into English were taught. It was attended by twenty-five pupils, the majority of whom were from the Sudra caste. Its support was largely drawn from English friends of the Mission cause in Guntur, at least half, who took a deep interest in this work. But the school was not destined to grow from this small beginning without serious interruptions.

During the early days of our occupation of the Rajahmundry field there was also a flourishing English school at that station, which, in 1858, under the Rev. Heise, reported eighty boys under instruction. In fact, in 1859, the Mission conducted *three* schools, in which English was made the medium of instruction, a third having been opened at Samulcotta. But all these schools had to be closed for lack of funds and missionary supervision, consequent upon the withdrawal of the Rev. Heise in 1851, and the death of Long in 1866; Samulcotta being closed in 1862, Rajahmundry and Guntur in 1862 or 1863.

Let us trace the history of the Guntur school more in detail. In 1857 the Indian Government made a proposition to the Mission at Guntur to establish an English school under government supervision as to its literary branches, offering Rs. 200 ($100) per month towards its maintenance, and making no restrictions in regard to religious instruction. But the executive committee declined the offer on the ground that it might lead to future complications and entanglement, and embarass the work. As we see matters now, that was a lost opportunity to get all higher education under Mission control. Already in 1853 the Hon. Mr. Stokes, the Mission's tried friend, in writing to the executive committee, said, "another felt want, which strikes me, is that of a man, who could give his time chiefly to the English school. If this were really efficient, I believe that the sons of all the richer natives would gradually avail themselves of it, and thus be brought within the sound of the Gospel." However, though urged both by the government and friends of the Mission, a splendid opportunity was let slip, and a strong rival government school was opened subsequently, which has in recent years been handed over to a local committee of Hindu gentlemen, and stands for the most approved and orthodox Hinduism. But, we, of course, do not refer to this by way of censuring any one; only from our present position, it seems as if we lost a very fair start on our Hindu rivals by not seizing the opportunity thus offered.

However, our Mission did follow the advice of Mr. Stokes; the old school continued on its existing basis from 1852 to 1854 under the Rev. W. I. Cutter. In 1858, when the Rev. Snyder was returned, his special duty was to manage and push forward the work of our English or Anglo-Vernacular school. But he had scarcely got fairly started in his work, when God called him home. After his death the Rev. E. Unangst, then just arrived, took charge of the school, and under him its standard and efficiency were raised. But even after this, for a time, this excellent work was destined to be closed.

The financial situation, incident to the great Civil War in the United States, became so serious that money could hardly be secured to maintain the missionary force. Much of their work had to be sacrificed to the stringency of the times, and the English school was closed. But it was never from any lack of confidence in this agency. He lamented, and so did the executive committee, the necessity of this step by which a most promising work was stopped in its very first success; for the growing popularity of the school was manifest, and its good work was realized, especially in the preparation of a grade of superior native assistants to enter the service of the Mission and to preach the gospel in the surrounding villages. It should also be noted that this step was made necessary by the withdrawal of many of the Mission's best English friends, through whose generosity the school had been kept up. For more than eleven years this field remained uncultivated. The government was not inactive during this period, but carried out its plan and opened an Anglo-Vernacular school, provided it with a good building and efficient staff. With this, as has been remarked, our chance of securing the control of all higher education was lost.

During this time, too, we must not forget that for five years *only one missionary* was left to look after the entire work. But the idea was never given up for a moment, and, in 1873, when a force of three missionaries was on the ground and the field had been narrowed down by the handing over of the Rajahmundry field to the General Council in 1869, it was again determined to open this work. In 1874 (February) the Rev. L. L. Uhl re-organized this work and "for a year," in the language of the Report of 1875, "this plan of presenting the truths of Christ to the higher classes of the Hindu community was carried out with marked encouragement." But its existence was seriously threatened at the start, for in 1875 the Board determined to close the school and send the principal to the Palnad to take up the "active" duties of the Mission field. It was resolved, "That the English department of the high school be discontinued, and that the Rev. Mr. Uhl be sent into the Palnad district, while the general supervision of the school be placed under the resident missionary at Guntur." But more sober counsels prevailed. The principal was asked to give reasons why the school should not be closed, which suffice it to say proving abundantly cogent, the work was continued. The school was started on a non-caste basis. All classes and castes were welcome to its benefits. Our Christian Boarding Boys were admitted. This gave great offense at first, and all high-caste pupils withdrew. They refused to occupy the same room and sit on the same seats with those whom they regarded as *outcaste*. Such was the condition of affairs in Guntur in 1874, indicating the strength of caste prejudice. Nevertheless the desire for education was so intense that by the end of the first month, the caste pupils had reconsidered the matter and there were twenty such in regular attendance, and by the close of the year there were eighty-five, of whom seventeen were Christian; in 1875 the number rose to one hundred and twenty-seven, of whom ninety-four came from the various Hindu castes and thirty-three were non-caste pupils. The different classes of the Hindu community reached by its influence may be better gathered from the following figures, which also include the Anglo-Vernacular primary schools, which are conducted for the same purpose and in the same way as the college of which they are feeders. We take the year 1890 as giving a fair average of the character or class of pupils attending the schools:

	Pupils in Attendance.	Christian.	Hindu.	Muhammedan.	Total.
1890	655	91	516	48	655

Of the Hindu boys under instruction not less than fifty per cent. belong to the Brahmin class, the intellectual and religious leaders of India; but all classes of this complex Hindu community are represented, and efforts are made to reach the most backward. The fact that this school and its branches are established for higher religious aims, and have been employed for the dissemination of Christian truths, has ever been maintained, and though it does militate against the popularity of the school to a certain extent, it remains true that the success of the schools has been remarkable, especially when the intense temper of the Hindu against a foreign faith is remembered. The report of the principal, in 1880, shows us the real struggle as it became manifest to him. "In each young man," he says, "remaining in the school four or five years, there has been a vast advance in his understanding of the gospel. I know of many young men who see and feel the folly of idolatry. But it is hard for a man to have all his foundations knocked away, and his hopes cut down. It is no easy thing for the soul to leave all it has clung to, and unreservedly give itself to what is new to it. * * * I know many young men who have been drawn towards Christ, and who say, if they believed Him God, they would accept Him. This is very precious."

In 1883, the Rev. L. B. Wolf joined the Mission, and became assistant principal. In January 1, 1885, he, on the retirement to America, on furlough, of the Rev. L. L. Uhl, became the principal. In September, 1885, the school was affiliated to the Madras University, and was made a second-grade college under the rules of the university. For the sake of those who do not understand the system of education, it may be well to state that the course of instruction in the Mission college comprises three years in the lower secondary department, three years in the upper secondary or high-school department, and two years in the college. In other words, an exceptionally *clever* lad has a course of eight years laid out for him, or with the four years in the primary or Anglo-Vernacular branch school, he has a twelve years' course open to him in our Mission. We say clever advisedly, for a system of examinations is in vogue in India which compels the majority of boys to repeat a year in each department, and not infrequently two. So it turns out that our schools practically have the training of young India from five years to twenty. What this means in development of the young men cannot be over-estimated. New thoughts are implanted, and a new life is set before them.

In 1881 a Sunday-school was organized in connection with the college, which has been carried on with much success to the present time. The attendance was made a part of the school work at first, but efforts have been put forth to make voluntary the attendance at its sessions, with commendable success.

CORNER-STONE OF ARTHUR G. WATTS' MEMORIAL COLLEGE.

The great work done for the College has been the securing of a permanent home for it, through the

ARTHUR G. WATTS, M. D., BALTIMORE, MD., U. S. A., BORN JANUARY 10, 1861, DIED JUNE 10, 1888.

energy of Dr. Uhl and the generosity of the kind people of America, seconded so nobly by the donation of the Messrs. Watts, whose gift has been acknowledged by making it a "memorial" to a dear son and brother, Arthur G. Watts. The Indian government through its educational department contributed Rs. 22,500 ($11,250) to this project. The building was constructed under the supervision of the principal, the Rev. L. B. Wolf. Ground was broken by his son, Geo. Brenner Wolf, June 27, 1889; the little hands which turned the first sod lay still in death * before a month had passed away. The corner-stone was laid by Mr. A. T. Arundel, the collector of the district, in the presence of a large concourse of people, on the 18th of March, 1890, and the building was formally opened by His Excellency, Lord Wenlock, the Governor of Madras, on the 17th of March, 1893. The building is of stone, a hard granitoid, and the wood-work is Burman teak. It is covered with Basel Mission tiles, and is provided with a hall, capable of seating four hundred persons. It has fourteen class-rooms and has accommodation for 400 students. It was first occupied by the College in October, 1893.

Our theological school is also under the same roof, and is in charge of the Rev. John Aberly. Those students who study only Telugu also recite with the college classes in some subjects, and are under the instruction of Rev. Aberly, assisted by sub-pastor N. Robert and O. Sivaramiah. The use of the building for this purpose is one of the chief ends which it subserves, and

---

* Geo. Benner Wolf died of cholera July 22, 1889.

LORD WENLOCK, GOVERNOR MADRAS PRESIDENCY, AND STAFF. MISSIONARIES, PROFESSORS AND STUDENTS, AT OPENING OF THE COLLEGE, MARCH 17, 1893.

for which it was constructed, and, as time goes on, it will yet serve a larger purpose. At present all instruction in our theological school is in Telugu, and is largely of an elementary nature, to suit the capacities of the students; Exegesis, Church History and Evidence of Christianity being the main subjects taught, with an effort, above all, to ground the boys in Biblical Theology.

The attempt is being made to encourage our students to read on in the College and prepare themselves to pursue their theological course in English. The evident advantage of this is that they would have ample opportunity to broaden their knowledge by the use of English books, while now they are almost entirely dependent on their teachers for all they get. This will be a great gain, when once it has been reached. As our Christian community develops in power and intelligence, there will be a larger number of lads who will push on into the higher classes in the College and read our best works in English.

The effort is persistently made to enlist the sympathies of our Hindu and Muhammedan boys in the truths of Christianity, by means of our Sunday-school and weekly Bible classes. They are thus taught a knowledge of Him who came to save the world from sin, and whose challenge, "which of you convinceth me of sin?" remains unanswered. It is this steady instruction, this study of Christ, whose character shines with such fearless splendor in this dark world, which must claim the allegiance of India some day; and the hope of the missionary is the blessed promise of the Master, "and I, if I be lifted up from the earth, will draw all men unto me."

THE ARTHUR G. WATTS' MEMORIAL COLLEGE BUILDING, APPROACHING COMPLETION.

The plan of thus instructing the rising generation of the land in Christian truths has a most encouraging future. While education brings about the disintegration of popular Hinduism, the land requires a Christian education to furnish the new principle of life, out of which a really great and enduring "New India" of the future must come. A development along any other lines must be looked upon with apprehension. Surely missionary societies cannot afford to stand by and see

THE ARTHUR G. WATTS' MEMORIAL COLLEGE BUILDING AT THE FORMAL OPENING, MARCH 17, 1893.

all the education in secular hands, or what is much worse, maintained by those who are hostile to Christianity. In this future India, now forming, there must go Christian thought and life, the highest thought and noblest aims of that faith which has won the first place among the most advanced peoples of the world. Education, controlled by the spirit and mind of Christ, must be depended upon in working out the future destiny of "New India." Surely the day should have gone by long ago when the missionary, in the college or high school, who has fairly grasped the great problem of India's educated classes, should be looked upon as doing a less real missionary service than he who labors in the district among the little growing congregations of humble Christians, or who spends his time in the bazaar among the masses. We must not forget the mighty work to be done for India in many directions, so as in its doing to have place, in the language of another, for "the preacher-missionary, the pastor-missionary, the translator-missionary, the author-missionary, the traveller-missionary, the doctor-missionary, the engineer-missionary, the artisan-missionary, the gardener-missionary, the secretary-missionary and the editor-missionary." These, one and all, are important, and if these why not the "education-missionary." Only so all keep in mind the *end, the making known of Christ.* He, above many of these, has a permanent place in which to influence young men in the most impressible period of life, and of teaching the "Life of lives" to those who stand in need of the certainty of Christianity and the mighty moral and spiritual power of Christ, the Son of God. Their education, unleavened by Christian principles, may prove to be the agent of their ruin and make it the powerful instrument by which they may work untold harm to those around them. We must keep our hands on the colleges and universities of the land, and make them more powerful and active agents in the dissemination of truth, in the overthrow of error and superstition, and the positive force through which the most powerful blows are to be dealt this hoary old faith.

CHAPTER IX.

ORGANIZATION CONTINUED.

Evangelization.

THE evangelistic work of a Mission is pre-eminently *the* work for which Missions have been organized. To bring Christ to the nations, to gather into His Church believers, to organize and develop those gathered into self-supporting and self-propagating centers of Christian thought and life amid the surrounding darkness of heathenism, is the first and chief task set the Church of Christ for its accomplishment. The means at hand to do this work are not only human, but human and divine; men having and believing the gospel themselves, and preaching it with power under the aid of the Holy Spirit to their fellowmen. A gospel, a most wonderful revelation of love and grace, has been committed to the Church, and with it a corresponding responsibility to make it known to others. With St. Paul, every true believer must needs say: "I am debtor both to the Greeks and to the barbarians: to wise and unwise." Preaching the gospel then is the chief work of the missionary and must occupy his most serious efforts. The evangelizing character of all Mission work needs no consideration, it has been remarked upon; but the distinction to be borne in mind is that all organization in the evangelistic branch, strictly speaking, is only that the gospel may be more successfully presented. The organization of this branch hence is of great importance, and on it, humanly speaking, will depend its effectiveness. The gospel, the power of God unto salvation, may be so unsystematically and irregularly preached as to bring few, if any, results. If then bazaar preaching be the plan adopted to reach the unevangelized masses, *i. e.*, open-air services in the market places, where people are wont to congregate at all times for purposes of trade or conversation, it must be persisted in at the same place and at regular intervals, so that by degrees a more or less permanent audience is secured. It has indeed been found a good plan to *rent* a room in the crowded part of the market, so that the work may be carried on without the annoyance of the noise and opposition which may prove a serious hindrance to it in the open market. Such plans of work are especially suited to large towns and cities. For work in the country a different organization is necessary. The missionary tent and bullock coach or country cart, along the canals the canal-boat or the horse, become his helps, protecting him from an Indian sun, and bearing him to his work among the outlying villages, where, with his native workers, he holds services among those who have placed themselves under his influence and instruction. Or he has open-air meetings in the village bazaar or near his tent, to which all are welcome. This work is hence a combination of strictly evangelistic effort to reach the heathen masses and the development of the little congregations of Christian people, who have professed Christ and been baptized. Unfortunately, the latter work has, in the case of most missionaries, become so burdensome as to leave very little time for the former, and the only way to manage this department is to increase the number of workmen and lessen the size of their fields of labor.

The beginning of these little congregations is extremely interesting. As soon as a little group of baptized Christians is found, the attempt is made to institute Christian worship, and provide them with the ordinary means of grace, the regular preaching of the word and the sacraments. Along with these methods of work go the distribution and sale of religious tracts and the Holy Scriptures, as well as the organization of the village school and Sunday-school.

Our Mission has tried all these methods in its evangelistic work. Our missionaries from the first preached in the market places, toured among the villages, spoke at stated times in the bazaars in rooms set apart for the purpose, and did all the work of an evangelist. In 1843, Revs. Heyer and Valet made a preaching tour through the Palnad Taluk, and impressed the mind of a man at Polepalli, who a year later came to Guntur, was given tracts, and early in 1847 was baptized, the first native Christian in that part of our field. His name was Malapati John. During the early years of our work preaching tours were organized in the district. In 1849, accounts are on record of tours made in the Palnad Taluk, and in 1853, H. Stokes, Esq., notices a long tour made by the missionaries with him through the western part of our field, participated in by the Revs. Heyer and Grönning and Mrs. Gunn and Mrs. Grönning. The same work was carried on in other parts of the field. The work of evangelizing was the only one that the missionary then had on his hands. Tending the flocks of gathered sheep was not a burden then, for the land was wholly given to idolatry, and Christ had been confessed by very few. Accounts of such work are numerous in the diary of the Rev. Gunn. But he laments that while he was carrying on the evangelistic work in the villages his work in the schools was neglected. Speaking of the tours in villages in 1848, six years after the Mission was started, he says that at Polepalli, where he had baptized John in 1847, while he addressed the people at one place, Mr. Beer, of Godaveri Delta Mission, spoke to a large audience in his tent, and their work continued on till 10 o'clock at night.

We have seen that this work progressed with the greatest rapidity in the Palnad Taluk, distant from Guntur more than sixty miles. To undertake the superintendence of this work with greater success, "Father Heyer" moved to that distant Taluk in 1849, where through the kindness and generosity of Mr. Stokes, a compound and bungalow were made over to the Mission, and for over three years, alone, with no

European resident nearer than Guntur, he pushed the work with great earnestness and success. But the hostile climate told even on his iron constitution, and, his health giving way in 1853, he was relieved by the Rev. Grönning, who took up the work and removed thither with his family.

But while the evangelistic work was pushed with so much success in the Palnad field it was not neglected elsewhere. In and around Guntur progress had been made; at Jonnalagadda the first baptism took place in 1849, a town six miles from Guntur. The man's name was Simeon (or rather that was the name given him at his baptism), while in the town of Guntur, within one year after his (Heyer's) arrival, he had baptized fourteen, including six adults. However, none of these were natives of Guntur, all having come thither as servants of English officials. The first baptisms in Guntur were a man and his wife in July, 1844. But the work, though small, was destined to grow, for in it were not only human prayers and efforts, but God's hand, divine love and promise; and under more systematic methods and with greater help and more efficient native workers, it has spread all over the field from these feeble beginnings—the fulfilment of His promise whose the work is, and the wonder of those who have all along doubted.

It may be said, without any exaggeration, that hardly as much effort is expended now to bring one hundred of these people to confess Christ in holy baptism as it took in those early days to bring *one* to that point; from the same class of the Hindu community the tendency is toward Christianity, and the great work is to instruct, train, discipline, in a word, organize these people into self-supporting and intelligent Christian congregations, with a Christian conscience, and with Christian notions of life, social, moral and spiritual, with all that this involves. God's word has certainly been blessed most richly; it has not "returned void," but it has accomplished that which He pleased, and prospered in the thing whereto He sent it.

The present organization may require a little more explanation. We have already seen how our Mission field is divided into Taluks for governmental purposes. These furnish us with the basis of our ecclesiastical divisions. Theoretically, within the borders of the Krishna district alone, we have seven sub-divisions or Taluks; and it has been our aim, if possible, to circumscribe a missionary's work within one of these Taluks. But such *intense* work, while commending itself to the best judgment of the missionary, has not been possible on account of the fewness of our laborers, and not infrequently it has happened that three, two and even *one*, have been the utmost at our command for this work. But this fact does not affect the organization; the plan is the same, and the end to be reached is to place a well-qualified man in each of these seven sub-divisions. The control and influence of this work will depend upon the frequency and strictness of the foreign supervision. The smaller the force, the less frequent will be the visits of the missionary, and the less his power for good. Our present staff enables us to put five men into this superintending work, and already the effects are manifest in larger benevolence and stricter discipline, both among native workers and congregations. Then too, it must not be forgotten that, when this evangelistic force is so small, little more can be done than the superintendence of the congregations. The great unreached and unevangelized mass, all around, must be passed by—must wait till the Church can make up its mind to send men to preach to them. No man, no missionary, with forty or fifty congregations, however small they may be, can do the work of an evangelist. "The care of the churches" is too absorbing. But on this point we cannot dwell, nor is there need. All see how inadequate is our force for all the work which ought to be done, and which must be done too, to fulfil Christ's great command.

Taking now the Taluk as the ecclesiastical unit for purposes of superintendence, within whose limits the foreign missionary exercises control, let us examine into the character of the organization more minutely. In this field the missionary is reigning bishop, and his word is law. He is subject, however, to such rules* in the management of his work as from time to time the Conference of all the missionaries may enact. His powers are limited by the combined powers of the missionary body, and he can only suggest rules for the better guidance of

* See Appendix.

the work, but cannot legislate himself for the people under him or his native assistants. Thus the work is unified, and the people are made to feel that back of the missionary, in all matters of discipline, there lies both a court of authority and appeal—an absolute necessity in such a land and among such people. Only once, thus far, has the authority of the Conference been set at defiance, and appeal made to the Foreign Mission Board in America, but with only one effect, to strengthen its authority among the people. The wisdom of such an organization for the management of our work has been demonstrated so often that no one who calmly looks into it can doubt its influence.

But its wisdom becomes more evident when it is kept in mind that under each missionary, in his ecclesiastical domain, there is a staff of native workers, sub-pastors, catechists, sub-catechists, helpers and school-teachers, to guide and control whom requires skill, tact, law and authority. At present, all receive their pay from foreign funds, and all collections made are paid into the Mission treasury, the only exception being that organized congregations are expected to assist in the support of the sub-catechist and school teacher, to whom the Mission gives only a limited salary. This plan has worked fairly well, but it is not by any means the last step that must be made. It can easily be seen that ability and, above all, grace and infinite patience are needed on the part of the missionary who would properly exercise rule among his assistants and make them understand the great responsibility of their position toward their fellowmen, so that they perform the part of good shepherds and not that of mere hirelings. Large spiritual capacity and ability to influence men—the power of the truth and the gift of the Holy Ghost—are essential for him who would train, as well as superintend, those workers placed under him. Great fidelity on his part, and a consciousness of his entire dependence on God, a prayerful, earnest life alone will make a man a real apostolic missionary, and not a mere agent of the home churches or a servant of the Boards.

Besides this superintendence of the workers, with the assistance of his catechists and sub-pastors, the missionary has his time greatly occupied in settling disputes in the congregations, examining candidates for baptism, inspecting the schools, admitting to church membership, and administering the holy communion to all those deemed worthy—in fine, having his eyes open to all that goes on not only among his assistants but in all the congregations. His chief helpers in this varied and arduous work are the sub-pastors and catechists—both classes forming our most trusty and intelligent workers, though not ordained to the regular work of the ministry, and hence not qualified to perform all ministerial acts. These men have charge of from one-third to one-half a Taluk and are constantly moving among the people, preaching to them, examining the schools and candidates for baptism, keeping the sub-catechists or village preachers up to their work, referring all disputes and ecclesiastical troubles to the missionary which they find they cannot themselves settle or which from their gravity should be settled by the missionary, and performing innumerable functions required by the work in its initial stages.

To the sub-catechist there are usually entrusted three or four villages, in which he holds services, instructs inquirers, and is in daily touch with the people. He is under the direct control of the catechist or sub-pastor, the efficiency of his work depending largely on the character of the control of those over him. He is supposed to be in such contact with the congregations and inquirers as to be able to give all needed information to his superiors when required. His work among the people will depend for its success in great measure upon the character of the man.

The helpers are those who have been employed to do the work of sub-catechists until better men can be prepared. They are usually a class of men who have considerable native ability but very meagre education, and are able to keep the congregations together, do a little elementary instruction, conduct services, and in many ways help to keep the people from lapsing into heathenism. We, as a Mission, have been compelled to use these men, though of very inferior training, in order to keep pace with the demands of our growing evangelistic or village congregational work. It is often the means used to gather in a village for which no other worker is available.

But from all this it must not be concluded that the idea of self-supporting congregations has been lost sight of, or that steps have not been taken looking toward the days when these village congregations shall have their own autonomy, select, under the guidance of the missionary, their own pastors and, as far as possible, support them. Already a plan is being roughly outlined of which we may mention the salient features. A number of congregations, two or three or more, depending on their size and contiguity, under the ministry of a sub-catechist, it is planned to develop into a charge, something after the organization at home. Pastors will be placed over them, whose business it will be to do all they can for their development, subject of course to the help and superintendence of the missionary, so long as he deems his oversight helpful and so long, at least, as foreign money is given in part payment of the native pastor's salary. We are contemplating moving in this direction, though it seems wise to hasten slowly, as men and congregations must be trained for and into this plan before the step is taken. In the great Church Missionary Society the plan to develop self-supporting congregations has been limited to forty years, and one-fortieth part of the support from the home funds is theoretically each year supposed to be withdrawn from the native congregations and raised among them every year. It is at least a plan that commends itself to the slow-moving native.

Poor as the people are, it is certain that they will be

able to do considerable toward the support of the pastors, and when properly-trained and earnest men can be secured, and the congregations taught to see how much it will be to their benefit to have their own pastors, the hope is not unwarranted that where now we have sub-catechists we will have a number of self-supporting or partly self-supporting charges. We are neither over-sanguine nor over-cautious in this matter as a Mission, and are trying to "hasten slowly," so that permanency and efficiency, with a true grounding in the truth, may result. A better grade of sub-catechists, men of more training and Christian experience, must be raised up for this. The people must be taught self-support as their bounden duty and highest privilege. To do this among our people is, of necessity, slow work, but it will come about, if only we can have wise superintendence and a permanent Foreign Staff.

We have now villages contiguous to each other where a pastorate could, with a fair expectation of success, be organized on the lines above indicated, and where at least a moiety of the salary might be raised. To encourage the people we must not ask too large a part at first, but anywhere from one-eighth to one-third would be a reasonable demand.

We have elsewhere spoken of the part played in our village work by the schools. They are taught in most part by the wives of our village workers and the young men from our boarding school who have not as yet been placed in charge of the regular village work. In some cases they perform the double office of school-teacher and Bible reader, *i. e.*, they conduct worship in the congregations on the Lord's day. However, this line of work, while carried on in some Missions to a considerable extent, has never been largely followed in our Mission; indeed, where the right men have been appointed as school-teachers, it is a plan which is worth a fair trial.

In training and developing this organized evangelistic staff, the missionary has another important function to perform which requires a brief notice. He lays down a course of study for all native workers, and conducts yearly examinations, on the results of which, with special reference to character and general efficiency, promotions are made to higher and more responsible duties, with better remuneration. No man is exempt from these examinations unless providentially hindered, and strict account is taken of all absentees. By this means the native workers are made more efficient and intelligent. Habits of reading and study are encouraged, and the process of pruning out the more inefficient ones is made possible. The principal subjects in which these examinations are conducted are biblical, though there are many practical questions asked on sanitation, congregational work and supervision, and in preaching to both Christians and Hindus, and the best methods to be followed in either case.

Now this may seem to some rather a complicated organization for evangelizing and organizing the

Church of Christ in India, and may seem to lack that apostolic simplicity which they find in the New Testament. But we believe, if carefully examined in the light of the peculiar circumstances of our Indian Church, it will recommend itself to any thoughtful mind as a very effective system. In the nature of the case the missionary, with his multifarious duties and extended field, cannot see his congregations more than two or three times a year, and can preach and administer the sacraments to them only on these tours of visitation.

The only way, at this stage of the work, by which his influence and superior knowledge, discipline and control can be made most effective, is by influencing and controlling those who constantly move among the people after the manner of our sub-catechists. In his monthly meeting with all his workers, the missionary has an opportunity to help the congregations by instructing their sub-catechists, who spend part of the time, at least, in learning how to do their work or in being taught what to teach. He is the best missionary who can multiply his influence by as many times as he has assistants, and who can put his spirit and the larger mind of Christ into the heart and work of his native workers. Now we need this system of work in this infant stage; by and by we shall be able to remove these scaffoldings and develop more and more a Church with its own autonomy, a self-supporting and self-propagating Church, which will need no foreign supervision or financial support, but which will carry on its own affairs and develop along those lines, which may be dictated by the national life and the oriental modes of Hindus.

God has blessed this organization. Through it the truth is being made known, and He will guide those who have the future in hand, so as not to let it hinder, but help in the establishment of an indigenous Church. What has already been done, through this organization, justifies us in the hope of yet greater things. The people are learning the truth, and by means of our congregational schools, the children are being trained in Christian thought, so that they will really, in intelligence, begin where their parents left off, experience excepted, and the future Church will have many whose intelligence will materially aid in that self-development and self-help toward which our efforts are constantly directed.

But we cannot pass from the consideration of the organization of our work without calling attention to the fact that the work thus organized is *one in aim and spirit*. It is only to bring the whole work of the Mission more clearly to view, that we have spoken of it as school, Zenana, medical, and evangelistic. Every department of the work is evangelistic, carried on to show the spirit of the gospel and to bring the truth home to all classes of the nation. Christ is the beginning and end of all effort, it matters not along what lines, as well as the motive and life of every department of the Mission. It is His life and example, His death and sacrifice, which alone point out the purpose of our work and give meaning to all that is undertaken. Experience has taught that the method may vary by which the truth may reach men, and that methods which fail elsewhere may be blessed to many under different circumstances.

No greater injury can accrue to the missionary cause than an attempt to set different methods of work in antagonism to one another, or advocate the one at the expense of the other. All combine in making up what experience has justified as a wise missionary administration of the Church's trust to this great people. The time should have passed, when men are so bent on the wisdom of their own special department of work as not to see the importance of each or the aim of the whole—how each part fits into and helps on the rest, and how all combine to form a solid movement against the various opposing forces. Educational work without Christ is only *negative;* with Christ it carries that positive element which must ever be found in the elevation of the whole man. Medical work without Christ is only sweet philanthropy; but with Christ, it has the seeds of eternal truth in its influence; and so with every part of this work, when permeated with the gospel of Christ, and done in His name and for His sake. The effect of all must mightily shake the dry bones of this nation until men and women begin to stand on their feet and lead new lives in His name and strength. Let there be an end of illiberal criticism of methods. Let all methods be subjected to a fair and impartial tribunal, and much of the misunderstandings and unrest will soon pass away. The enemy is too strong for the missionary army to spend much time or strength in disputes about methods among the different arms of the service. Let every part of the army march as near to the Captain as possible, and carry out His great command, in season and out of season, and He will honor and crown with success the effort of the faithful, it matters not to which department of the missionary host one belongs.

CHAPTER X.

PROGRESS.

General Considerations — Negative Results — Indian Field only Old Question — Our Mission Progress, Numerical — Mental — Moral — Spiritual.

THE progress of any cause from its rise to the height of its prosperity is a question considered with great eagerness by both friends and foes. It is a burning question in Missions. The mathematician has been at work here and shown, to his entire satisfaction either the utter futility of the attempt to gather in the nations, or the rapidity of the work and its speedy accomplishment. We must, in the question, remember a few general facts. It is true that the gospel has only partially changed the life and habits of those nations among which it has been preached now these thousands of years. We are wont to speak of the nations as *nominally* Christian; of heathen at home; of the unreached masses in Christian lands. It is unnecessary to emphasize the fact that there are many thousands in Christian lands who bow the knee to Baal and kiss his image. This is only another way of putting the truth that, under the most favorable circumstances, there have been many who have not confessed Jesus Christ. However, He has hold of the nations' conscience, the laws and their execution, social habits and customs—the whole life of the nations is under the control of the principle of the Nazarene. He rules in the councils of states, and, though not always ascendant, His ascendency becomes more and more a recognized fact. Thus must we view Christian progress among those nations in which Christian thought and life have been longest prevalent.

How stands the matter in those nations in which Christ has been known only a few hundred years; and that too very imperfectly in the nature of the case? We have already observed that the Roman Catholic Missions are only 350 years old, and the Protestant scarcely 200. What has been the progress; what have been the victories? Progress is not easily grasped in such a work. There is a progress that cannot be put in a tabular form, which is nevertheless one of the main considerations in the question of a fair estimate. The stages of *preparation* for Christ were quite as important in God's plan of grace for the world as were those periods immediately following Christ's birth. For 2000 and more years the world was in preparation for the gospel—Christ's advent; for thirty years after, the world waited for his manhood years, and for the hundreds thereafter many nations have waited for Him to be preached to them; yet no one would say that all these years have not been years of preparation, perhaps negative, yet preparation of a kind that cannot be overlooked in the final summing of the progress of Christ through the nations. So too the years spent in quiet preparatory work in sowing the seed of the kingdom, the silent working of the truth through the ages before it is fully grasped or admitted, the breaking down of the old barriers to faith, and the change to the *new*—this time, and the effect of this working, have a most important part in the question of Christian progress, and are factors which no fair estimate of the influence of Christ through the ages can disregard.

How stands this question in India? It has recently been subjected to a critical review by an English Canon. We have briefly in an opening chapter shown the peculiarity of the situation, and the many hindrances in the way of progress, many of which are not found among aboriginal or barbarian tribes. To a certain extent, elements enter into the question of Indian evangelization which perhaps are more difficult to overcome than those among aboriginal or barbarous tribes. We have not examined these difficulties exhaustively, yet they do contain certain elements peculiar to Indian evangelization. And yet we would not forget that while there are hindrances to the progress of the truth in India, which may not be found in the same form elsewhere, the tenacity with which men cling to old customs and old faiths is not so much because of the strength of those beliefs as because they have been believed and followed for a long time. Customs become religion, as all find who have lived among the old nations of the world. It is true the caste system is peculiar to India, yet we believe that the monotheism of the Muhammadans, or the ancestral worship of the Chinese, furnish as effectual barriers to the new faith in Christ. We are hence inclined to hold that we have rather a normal condition of things which presents, it is true, many and serious difficulties, but no more so than those which have always met and always will meet the onward progress of a new faith.

Progress, then, in Indian evangelization is hardly a new problem to the Christian statistician. It must be examined in the light of the past. The history of the Church will, through the ages, help materially to a satisfactory solution. If some of our modern critics had been dropped down into the Roman Empire in the first or second century, we are sure we should have heard them uttering the same blunders in regard to the progress of Christianity, which they now utter. "What a failure! How disappointing! How imperfect! How slow the progress! What a sad state of things do we find?" But after all we do not presume to know more about this matter than others, we only know that to the Church of Christ a message has been entrusted to the nations, and one which has the divine promise of ultimate triumph. It is not ours to reason when this shall be, or grow discouraged over the slowness of the movement!

If we cannot encourage ourselves in this work by any grand results or brilliant victories, we can, one and all, fall back on our great Leader, claim His promises and sing His hosannas, who has the great enterprise in His control, and who is Lord of hosts and will "lead captivity captive."

We turn to examine the progress we have made, fully recognizing that it is of God and humbly trusting that it may not be done in the spirit of self-glorification.

TELUGU CONGREGATION, GUNTUR.

A king had cause to repent once that he numbered his hosts; we do so, hoping that it may please God to accept it as intended to stir up these who have not been interested in this work and to encourage those who have been in the forefront of the struggle, and who by prayer and gifts have stood by the Mission through its history.

The numerical progress of our Mission first demands attention. Mathematics in Missions may be a dangerous science, but we venture to employ it with this caution, that it must not be utilized for the future. Mathematics in the hands of a prophet becomes a very dangerous weapon; by it, the world can be evangelized in this country yet. "Figures do not lie" is a good maxim, but it had much better read, Figures do not always tell the whole truth and nothing but the truth; yet there is a mighty encouragement to be gotten out of missionary mathematics. We as a Mission have had our little beginning, let us trace the numerical results. The table following will be instructive, showing how we gained ground through the years past:

PROGRESS. 275

Years.	No. of Villages in which Converts Live.	No. of Children in the Schools.	No. of Baptized Christians.	No. of Communicants.	No. of Children in Boarding Schools.	No. of Schools.	No. of School Teachers.	Workers all told, Native and European.	Remarks.
1843 (end of 1st year)	1	nil.	5	nil.	nil.	nil.	nil.	1	Children in the service of officials.
1848	5	133	43	*	*	4	4	(b) 7	(b) 3 Europeans.
1855	10	355	(a) 118	86	15	24	24	(c) 31	(c) 9 Europeans.
1860	14	485	(a) 206	110	*	22	22	(d) 37	(d) 6 Europeans.
1865	*	295	(a) 761	293	*	21	20	(e) 29	(e) 5 Europeans.
1870	39	443	1345	304	*	30	29	(f) 39	(f) 1 European. Represents G. S. M.
1875	105	312	2835	1254	36	17	22	65	
1880	223	1279	5423	2193	54	53	67	105	
1885	302	2094	8638	4789	144	145	147	247	
1890	371	4612	13566	7952	166	221	231	467	

* Not determined.   (a) Includes the Rajahmundry field.

This showing is at least encouraging, though any one who has dealt with the masses by which he finds himself surrounded, recognizes that it is only a drop in this great sea of humanity. We have shown in a previous chapter that the population of the seven Taluks in which our Mission has labored was over 800,000 in 1891, and compared with this, our numerical results seem very small. Yet we must not despise the day of small things. The few thousands are growing and will eventually reach and pass the first hundred thousand. Look at the leap in numbers between 1870 and 1880. There was an increase in the baptized members of over 300 per cent., and in the next decade over 168 per cent. The increase of the population in the Krishna district in the last decade was about 19 per cent., while the increase in the Christian population was almost 100 per cent., and in our Mission over 168 per cent. A review of Mission statistics develops the fact that the native Christian community doubles itself every decade. If the same rate of increase were to continue in that class of the community among whose members our Mission has been most successful, the whole of the outcaste population would be gathered into the Church *within thirty years;* but as intimated before, such prophecies are not to be depended upon, and do more harm than good. There are great barriers of caste, which make any calculation of this sort most unreliable. Thirty years may pass before any great advancement will be made among the solid Hindu unit, above our native Christian in the social scale..

This leads us naturally to show from what class this ingathering has come. Here we must be careful. God is no respecter of persons. These artificial distinctions of caste are man-made, but we must not close our eyes, in estimating progress, to the fact that the higher in the scale of civilization and worldly prosperity a people is, the more difficult it is to reach them with the

A GROUP OF CHRISTIANS, GUNTUR.

gospel. The common people heard Christ gladly. In India the same has been experienced, until the gospel has come to be regarded as a very good thing for the humble and outcaste, but as quite unnecessary to the great Hindu community. There is no occasion for discouragement in this. The principles of Christianity have never yet failed to lift up the lowly. From the slaves in Cæsar's household to the throne of the emperor, was not so great a distance as we are apt to think. Christianity has always begun among the lowly and outcaste, but it has never remained there; or perhaps it were better to say, it never allowed those who embraced it to remain long in obscurity. It is a religion which has been tested by the ages and has never failed to ele-

REV. DR UNANGST AND N. ROBERT, REVISING THE TELUGU BIBLE.

vate—morally, socially, spiritually—the whole man. This numerical showing then cannot be fairly understood unless it is remembered that the great bulk (ninety-nine per cent. is not too high an estimate), is from the Hindu standpoint regarded as the dregs of the nation—the out-castes.

The effort to lift them up has been fully joined. The intelligence of the class from which our Christians have come, might fairly be represented by zero in 1842. But the last fifty years have wrought an astonishing change, as the foregoing tabular statement shows; with such numbers in our schools, rapid progress has been made in the intellectual status of the people; and while thousands of them cannot read and write, yet there are always those at hand to help them in such matters as require assistance, in order to enable them to get their rights. The increase in the number of schools since 1880 of over 400 per cent., and almost the same in the number of school teachers, presents an encouraging picture for the future, and to us denotes great progress. It is certain that the class from which the members of our church have come is being more rapidly educated than any other class except the Brahmin; and what is most cheering, both boys and girls are reading in our schools in fair proportion. Mental advance can only be shown by the prevalence of schools, the regularity of attendance, and, where this standard is observed in the case of our native Christian community, it is certain there is great reason for hope, especially in primary education. Every effort must be made to improve the condition of these schools, and to get the people to appreciate them, as they too often unfortunately fail to do. But in the advancement of our Christian community, the school has played so prominent a part as to force itself upon our people's attention, giving our work both depth and permanency. To educate children out of heathenism is the way to raise up a strong Christian Church, and an informed community will soon show the fruits of their intellectual advancement in improved surroundings and higher aims in life.

But we must go one step further. Moral and spir-

A GROUP OF CHRISTIANS, GUNTUR.

itual progress is the hardest to estimate, but the most important. *For it*, all the rest exists. The end to be reached is *character*. No more frequent question is asked in the home-land than the one relating to the spiritual fruits, to character and life. Numbers are felt to be uncertain tests of the character of Mission work. Schools and colleges—the intellectual, industrial, mechanical, philanthropic advancement—the general spread of new ideas, and the adoption of our Western customs and civilization all are regarded as encouraging signs of the influence of Missions in these Eastern lands, but they do not satisfy the test as to life and character. To most persons the falling into one or the other of two dangers is almost inevitable, either to expect too much or to be too easily satisfied. Coming from lands with a Christian civilization and a religious life of centuries, it is very easy to forget how things have grown into their present state; while on the other hand, viewing results from the standard of surrounding heathenism or in comparison with it, there is danger of being too easily satisfied with what has been accomplished. We believe, however, that the experience of those who know the life and morals of oriental lands from a long residence, is unanimous in its declaration that the fruits of mission work are encouraging. It is true, the old faiths have a happy way of divorcing morals and life, and it often happens that this leaven works much harm in the Christian community; yet the piety and deep spiritual life of many of the humblest of those who have but cast away their idols are ample proofs of the power of the gospel and the genuineness of the work. We must not expect to find more unselfishness, less lying and thieving, a higher state of morals and a purity which do not exist in lands where Christ has been known for centuries. We are just in the beginning of an infant church-life, and while God by His spirit and grace can lift men above their surroundings, out of their past environment, nay, make a new one for them, it is evident that He still allows men "to work out their own salvation with fear and trembling," and encourages them to grow up into the perfect stature of Christ Jesus. Moral and spiritual fruits—progress in the formation of character and the realization of the Christ-life in the soul—must not be expected except by long and persistent effort, patient teaching and prayer. The Holy Spirit must take the things of Christ and speak with power to human souls. His work has been felt, and we can only wait on Him for larger measures of blessing—for a more abundant outpouring of His grace. We are conscious that we have done very little toward answering the question as to the spiritual fruit which has been reaped, but we are equally conscious that we are only able to estimate imperfectly what this is. Only God, the searcher of hearts, can tell what it is. We would err most egregiously were we to speak in glowing terms of the ripe fruits of spiritual life and character, as the manner of some is. So too we would be unwarranted in withholding the word of honest commendation which the genuine life of many deserves. The more we know of the sink of heathenism from which men have been rescued, the more highly we are bound to regard those who have escaped therefrom. The miracle of grace is constantly wrought in these lands, and to God be all the glory. Amen. It is enough to know that the way for Christ is being made in India and that thousands are on it. The missionary can only hold fast to the promises of a faithful God, amid this worse than Egyptian darkness, and help one here and encourage one there, here rebuke and there succor, filled with the spirit of the Master and confident that He shall drive away all night—all sin—and in His wake, truth, light, holiness shall arise.

In self-support what progress has been made? This is a question of no little interest. In the home lands it is pressing for answer, and many are disposed to think the missionary rather slow in urging it for practical answer. In India the question is a different one, owing to peculiar circumstances and the condition of the classes reached by Christianity. Theoretically, it would seem that there is no reason why the Indian church should not support itself, and yet, practically, there are many reasons why it cannot do so. Our Mission has made some progress here. The examination of finances of the Missions for the past two decades shows the following:

	Amount expended on the work in decade.	Amount contributed in India in decade.
1873 to 1883	$133,186.90	$10,905.57
1883 to 1893	$375,204.33	$65,995.00

It were easy to follow out the line of research here which the commercial spirit of the age has found so congenial in some circles, and estimate the cost of each baptized member; but such a use of this statement we leave to those who want everything put down in dollars and cents; we have quoted these figures to show that we are making *progress* in self-support on its financial side, for whereas in the first decade the amount contributed from all sources in India was only 8 per cent. of that expended, during the second decade it was over 17 per cent., or six times as much was received during the latter period as during the former, a good showing. Of course, we do not disguise the fact that much of this was not received directly from the people, but came in the shape of grants to the schools, and yet this does not affect the general question, and it remains settled that our work has received this financial encouragement from India. It should also be borne in mind that this represents only cash received, and does not show the benevolence *in kind*, which is quite an item of late years in all our reports; it being estimated at $1,000 in 1893. If it were added to the above amount contributed it would raise the percentage to 21 per cent. of the whole expenditure, or *would show that about one-fifth of all money spent has been received in India.* This should encourage those who seek after a sign! But self-support means more than money. It were superficial to take this alone into consideration.

We have been developing also in other lines which are quite as important. "What would be the result were the Missionary to withdraw from India at this time?"

one might ask. Well, we trust such a condition may never need to be faced, but still we venture to say what may seem more like prophecy than history, and yet it is based on what has gone before, that there has been such an impression made in the minds of the most thoughtful that there would not be wanting many who would take up the work and carry it forward under the truth and with dependence on the Spirit. This is a self-support which counts for more than the money item. There would certainly be a great change in the method employed, and it might, in places, fail for a time. Yet we believe the word of truth has taken such a hold of many that there would arise leaders in all parts to carry forward the work begun. The progress made in raising up men who are equipped for self-development and for efficient work among their countrymen, is the most encouraging part of the Missionary's work.; and though he is often wont to complain of the weak and inefficient worker, he can always, as one lately said in the hearing of the writer, find those among his assistants in the great work whom he views with pleasure and whose work is his constant joy. This by no means is intended to convey the idea that were the financial conditions of self-support fulfilled, the men would be ready to assume the more important responsibility of church management and development. All we wish to convey is that their progress there is real and solid, the more so too when one remembers the odds against which every effort must be made in such surroundings.

In general there is progress enough to encourage an active, earnest soul—hardly enough to bear aloft him who passes through Baca. A healthy faith and a hopeful spirit can see much to bring sunshine into his darkest day. The Church should catch all the inspiration she can from success already realized, but she should never allow herself to measure her zeal or gifts by the success which has attended her efforts. Only a proper

A NATIVE CHRISTIAN FEAST, CHRISTMAS DAY.

apprehension of the purpose of the gospel, a clear view of Christ's life and the example of holy men in the past, should hold her to her task. Success, however brilliant, will not do for her. What Christ has done gives her both a motive from which to act, free from all dross, and an end to be attained as high and holy as was His who "saved not himself" that He *might deliver man.*

We cannot finish this chapter in a more appropriate way than by quoting from the leading native Christian journal in South India, the *Christian Patriot.* In an editorial on "The Development of the Native Church," the editor says: "We thank God for the few here and there who live Christ-like lives, who realize their responsibilities as followers of Christ." Further on he says: "Compared with some of the other communities, ours is far in advance in the matter of education. Our females are better educated than those of any other class. In the matter of higher education we come next to the Brahmins, but notwithstanding this, it is a fact that there is a great lack of intellectual life and vigor in the native Christian community." This fairly represents what may be found in all missions, and all we would add is that our primary schools are our hope for the future, by means of which true knowledge and true religion will combine and develop into a strong, active India Church, filled with the truth and led by the Spirit, who will "sanctify her through the truth."

CHAPTER XI.

PROSPECTS—CONCLUSIONS.

WE do not forget that the offices of the historian and seer are quite distinct, and yet we propose to play the role of the latter even at the risk of being inconsistent. We have endeavored in the foregoing pages to record faithfully what has transpired in our Mission during the first fifty years of its history. What are the indications of the work for the future? What prospects are warranted by the past? We shall briefly summarize, rather than discuss, what we believe lies before us.

The first sign of encouragement with which we begin our second fifty years is a more friendly relationship with one of our sister Missions, the American Baptist Mission, with which we have for over a decade and a half been on rather strained terms. It would do little good to write up the history of the long controversy and all that transpired in the past relations of the two Missions; it is sufficient to know that matters have been adjusted in such a way that harmony must result between the Missions if there be a desire for it. No arrangement of the nature of the compromise of January, 1893, appointing a Board or committee of advisers between the two Missions on all questions of difficulty arising, can ever be effective or work out the ends which were had in view, unless there is an earnest desire to keep the peace for Christ and His gospel's sake.

With the field open to both Missions, it is inevitable that troubles will arise; but all these can with grace and patience be met and settled, if only the spirit shown at Vinukonda be present among the brethren of both Missions. If the brethren could have met in 1880 instead of 1893, much of the friction of the past would have been avoided and there would have been no "Protest and Appeal," which Dr. Downie seems to think so unnecessary in his history of the Telugu Mission (Baptist). But we would remind Dr. Downie that it is history that the opening of the Guntur Station, in 1842, was with the consent and approval of the Church Missionary Society brethren at Masulipatam, and at the special request of Collector Stokes, who had urged the Church Missionary Society to make Guntur a head station before our founder arrived; and for fifty years we have had unbroken harmony with these missionaries. Hence, no "protest." We divided the land and tried to respect each other's rights and honor each other's work. We fail to appreciate the position he assumes toward our "Protest" in 1883, but that must only be expected, as Dr. Downie, 140 miles away from our borders, can have only a very faint conception of the trouble and annoyance which the settling of the Mission in the Krishna district from 1880 to 1886 occasioned. However the agreement arrived at at Vinukonda is the beginning of better things. Mutually it was agreed not to receive each other's members or workers without a reference to, and the consent of the Mission to which they belong. It is true that no territorial limits could be agreed upon, but a board of reference consisting of two Missionaries for each Mission was recommended to our respective Home Boards and has since been ratified by them, and it is not too much to hope that the end of our unpleasant relations has been reached. This is a most cheering prospect.

Another indication of future success is the increase in our foreign staff. We have always been too few. But we begin the second half of the first century with encouraging prospects. The church at home has caught a clearer view of our work, and men are not wanting who are willing to devote themselves to this work. A new impulse has been given to the work, and we are soon within sight of a Missionary for each part of the field. But there is great need for enlargement in this direction, and the Mission can not be said to be fully manned until at least ten men, besides a full corps of lady Missionaries, are in the field. Still the prospect is encouraging, and the Church has reason to take heart, though much remains yet to be done before the Foreign Staff has reached that strength which the work requires.

The influence and position which fifty years of steady work have secured for us warrants us in forecasting a larger influence and a firmer position among the people. Confidence has been gained in the continuity of our

Mission and its institutions. The stage of doubt has passed away. Men have reason to believe that we have established ourselves here and propose to stay. Our influence is being felt among all classes, and we no longer need assure them that we are a permanent force which must be counted on in the future advancement and development of the community. Hence, it is easy to see that we have secured a position which is bound to claim more respect and which is sure to bring a larger influence. Without ostentation we have quietly worked on until all know that we are the friends of right and truth, the helpers of the poor and despised, the patrons of learning, the defenders of the defenceless; in a word that no cause, however insignificant, if right, fails to reach and influence us. Along a thousand channels our influence is spreading and our position is gaining strength, because it is not our undertaking on which we are bent, but His whose will is that all men may come to the knowledge of the truth.

Our hope is clear as the truth itself. God has not sent His servants on the errand of making disciples of all nations without the most definite instructions, coupled with the clearest promises of ultimate success. The prospects of our Mission are as certain and assuring as are the promises of God. Its success is insured in the promises of the "all men" for whom Christ died. Our vision cannot be brighter, hence, for the future of our work than God's promises. But as clear as is the promise and the prophecy of Him whom we preach, so sure is the hope that our labors in Christ will eventually result in the overthrow of heathenism and the establishment of the Cross in this great land. Our prospects brighten in the blessed promises of Christ, and we are filled with hope.

Fifty years and their record have closed. The sky is bright. God's hand has been over His church's planting. He will give the increase. The Christ, lifted up "upon the cross," must be preached, and all men will be drawn to Him. His mighty hand alone will bring the victory. He will raise up the instruments in India and in other lands through which He will accomplish His purposes of grace. His church must listen to his voice commanding her *to go*, and men and women must heed His call. The kingdoms of this world must become the kingdom of the Lord and His Christ, and He who is over all and above all will bring the end to pass in His own time. We can only wait on Him and do His will. India must be made ready for the King. Her King is ready, and will ascend His throne and be crowned Lord of all. For this great day we pray and labor and wait.

> "Jesus shall reign where'er the sun
> Does his successive journeys run."

"And I, if I be lifted up from the earth, will draw all men unto me."

Even so, come, Lord Jesus, "for Thine is the kingdom, and power, and glory. Amen."

APPENDIX I.

1842--1892.

BY REV. L. L. UHL, PH. D.

JUBILEE TOUR.

ON the 31st of July, 1842, Rev. C. F. Heyer—"Father Heyer," as he came to be called—ended in Guntur, India, a long journey which he had begun at Boston, U. S. A., Oct. 14, 1841. The time came for the celebration of the Jubilee of the Founding of the Mission, but because of the threatening famine of 1892 this celebration was postponed so as to be completed before July 31st, 1893. The day of little things had been superseded by that of great things in the Mission, the few of the beginning years had now become thousands, and it was with hope and enthusiasm that the Jubilee was finally entered upon on March 2d and 3d, 1893. These two days were the public beginning of the Jubilee, although much preparation was made beforehand. Revs. Uhl and Aberly and Dr. Anna S. Kugler had been constituted a committee of arrangements; it was resolved to attempt to raise Rs. 11,000, payable on subscription, with which to build a dormitory for the boarding boys, in memory of "Father Heyer;" a tour over the whole Mission by as many of the ladies and gentlemen as possible was planned; a choir of four male voices, Murári David, Jonnakóti Cornelius, Chikkála Joseph and Sudarsina Luke and one female voice, S. Meenakshi, was selected and trained; four Jubilee Hymns were composed, two extensive dialogues on the history of the Mission were prepared, and historical and practical subjects, covering the fifty years, were assigned to various missionaries, both ladies and gentlemen, as subjects of addresses; a large picture of "Father Heyer" was ordered; the whole matter talked over and written up, and the day for a general meeting at Guntur appointed. To this meeting all the workers and representatives from each congregation were invited, free entertainment was promised to all who should come. For this meeting tickets had been printed, a large pavilion erected, other accommodations provided, and the eating arrangements completed. Jerripotu Samuel Garu provided the pavilion and the food. March 3d may be taken as historically the opening day, when two monster meetings were held in the pavilion, perhaps the largest ever erected in Guntur. Forming in a procession at the new college building, the missionaries marched to the platform, while the audience which had collected together, numbered more than 1200 people, and was an inspiring Jubilee sight. Enthusiasm marked all the exercises, and when the day was over we counted by our lanterns a total subscription and collection of Rs. 4,045-0-1 ($2322.50). The day's work was a noble one, fit fruitage of fifty years toil.

With the rose is ever the thorn, and nothing so saddens one among the memories of that day as the deplorable superabounding of caste. The Christians of Mádiga extraction for two days protested that all arrangement for the food was in the hands of Christians of Mála extraction, vast numbers of them refused to partake on the first day, and on the second some of them went home without either food or Jubilee. This shows the almost deathless nature of caste feeling even among our Christians of non-caste origin. J. Samuel Garu reported an average of 680 persons daily entertained, while 780 complete tickets were issued.

THE PROGRAM OF THE TWO MEETINGS IS HERE GIVEN.

4TH MARCH, 1893, 8 A. M.

DR. UNANGST IN THE CHAIR.
    Proclamation—Rev. Uhl.
    Opening Service—Miss Sadtler at the organ.
    Scripture Reading—Sub-pastor Peravalli Abraham.
    Prayer—Rev. Uhl.
    Recitation—"Heyer's coming."
    Address, "Progress of the mission "—Rev. Aberly.
    Hymn, "Progress of the mission."
    Address, "The Jubilee "—Dr. Albrecht.
    Address, "Our Schools "—Rev. Wolf.
    Dialogue—"The History of the Mission."
    Address, "The money given by America in the fifty years "—Dr. Unangst.
    Address, "The money given by India in the fifty years "—Rev. Uhl.
    Hymn—"The A. E. L. Mission."
    Doxology and Benediction.

4TH MARCH, 1894, 5 P. M.

REV. WOLF IN THE CHAIR.
  Opening Service—Miss Sadtler at the organ.
  Scripture Reading—Rev. Aberly.
  Prayer—O. Sivaramayya Garu.
  Address, "Reminiscences"—Rev. M. Nathaniel.
  Address "The Jubilee"—Catechist Dasari Daniel.
  Dialogue.
  Hymn—"Founding of the Mission."
  Address, "More to be done for the Future"—Sub-pastor Peravalli Abraham.
  Address "Thank Offerings"—Sub-pastor Neelam Robert.
  Taking of Subscriptions.
  Hymn—"Gratitude."
  Benediction.

On March 4th began the tour throughout the leading congregations of the mission. The members joining regularly in this tour were the Misses Dryden and Sadtler, Revs. Unangst, Uhl, Albrecht, Aberly, Sub-pastor N. Robert and choir already mentioned. Others joining at times in the tour were Dr. Anna S. Kugler, Miss S. Home and Revs. Wolf and Yeiser.

It was evening at the village of Mèdakondùru, eleven miles from Guntur, when the first jubilee exercise of the tour was held. All arrangements of camp, travel and table were under control of Revs. Unangst and Uhl, who managed these on alternate days. In this way one set of tents and bandies would be occupied while another would be moving on to the next rendezvous. Imagine the meeting place an open space among the Christians' houses, with lanterns and torches to light up the scene, the people in a dense semi-circular mass on mats, straw, on the earth, the party of the tour on their chairs or mats in front with the tables and the baby organ, and you have an idea of the first village jubilee held—typical of all ordinary evening meetings of the tour. Villagers or caste people came around, non-Christians thronged about, and the interest was intense throughout. The collections and subscriptions amounted to Rs. 35-0-3 ($17.51), which all regarded a success.

The program of exercises at this place was, with slight variations, that commonly carried out in the evenings, and is here given:
  English and Telugu Hymns.
  Opening Exercises—Miss Sadtler at the organ.

Scripture Reading and Prayer.
Address, "The Jubilee"—Dr. Albrecht.
Hymn—"Heyer," with the crayon picture.
Address, "The Missionaries"—Sub-pastor N. Robert.
Dialogue—"Progress of the Mission."
Hymn—"Progress of the Mission."
Address, "Development of the Work"—Rev. Aberly.
Addresses, "The Women's Part"—Misses Dryden and Sadtler.
Hymn—"The Missionaries."
Address, "The Gifts from America"—Dr. Unangst.
Address, "The Gifts from the Mission Field"—Rev. Uhl.
Subscriptions.
Hymn—"The A. E. L. Mission."
Doxology and Benediction.

On the morning of the second day began the system of dividing and holding branch Jubilee exercises and then re-uniting at the next camp. Four horsemen, accompanied by the male singers, visited two villages and took up subscriptions, while the senior missionary, the ladies and female singer, wended their slow way in bandies to the next camp. This was a representative forenoon's work at the beginning of the Jubilee tours.

On the second day, the evening meeting was with the large congregation at Panidam and was marked with three new features. The first was the use of the magic lantern, causing the intensest interest and delight to the people. This exhibition, however, took so much time that it was given afterwards at only a few places. The second new feature at Panidam was the crayon of "Father Heyer," nearly life size, in a neat frame, just received from Messrs. Wiele & Klein of Madras. Most of the people visited on the tour had not before seen a picture, and showed the keenest interest in surveying this crayon. Men, women and children stared at it with bated breath and wide open eyes. Thousands have raised clasped hands before them, as if in worship of it. Audiences have been as but one person, the multitude of eyes as but one eye, before that wondrous picture! The third new feature at Panidam was the securing of a large subscription. The sum was much exceeded afterwards by even smaller congregations, and there is no doubt that this congregation would have given more largely had it had the stimulus of a visit towards the end of the tour and after others had given largely. As it was, these people did very well indeed and subscribed Rs. 147 ($73.50).

On the fourth day out, while the bandies were detouring about the Belamkónda Heights to reach Nandirájapálem and the horsemen were holding their accustomed meetings, the one at Dodléru was marked by the presence of village or caste people as regular members of the audience and regular subscribers. The Komma caste people here outnumbered the Christians, one of them contributed Rs. 17 ($8.50), another put down Rs. 5 ($2.50), and all showed much sympathy for the work. This co-operation of the caste people, especially of the farmers and village officials, was a marked feature in a number of Jubilee meetings. Subscriptions were made by these non-Christian villagers at Narasarowpett, Perála, Kunkalamiru, Manduru, Yedlapalli, Nevalikallu, Dharanakorta, Lingapúram and Balasapádu. At Nevalikallu they made an offering of Rs. 46-2-0 ($23.06), at Dharanakorta the Munsiff from Parasa gave Rs. 50 ($25), at Lingapúram they gave Rs. 111-6-0 ($55.80) while at the meeting in the very heart of the village of Balasapàdu Christians and villagers vied with each other as to who could contribute the larger sum. These nine places, besides others, where the caste people mingled with us in our Jubilee, form an earnest of better days to come for those people, their wives and their little ones.

On the fifth day out, having crossed the Sattenapalli Taluk (county), in a short cut of about thirty-six miles, as the camp went, we entered the Palnád Taluk, holding our first meeting at Pilutla and Pedugurála. The Pilutla people did nobly and made up a sum of Rs. 73-10-6 ($36.80).

It often happened in these tours, and for various reasons, that long daily journeys had to be made. The most notable of these was one of twenty miles over fields and rough ways, another of twenty-one miles, one more from Rentachintala to Tangedu of twenty-three miles, partly through stony and jungly tracks, and yet another of twenty-nine miles from Karempudi, though on good roads, the morning and evening meetings being kept up all the time. Most of these long trips were in the Palnád; the ladies endured bravely what is seldom undertaken by their sex, while the gentlemen, the servants and even the oxen came in for a mention of their patience and steadfastness in the heat and over bad roads.

After leaving Dachapalli, and on the seventh day out, we begun to tread on historical ground and to meet the scenes of the earliest work of the mission. Meetings were held at Atmakúru and Bódlavèdu, where the first Christians were baptized in 1850; at Veldurti, where the first turning to Christ was in 1849; at Durjál, among the very houses whose inmates sought our faith in 1848, and near Polapalli, where the first ingathering from the villages took place in 1847. It was much like being with "Father Heyer" living and partaking of the doings of forty-six years ago, to move among these places in the Jubilee.

At the same time that we were entering these historical places, there came a change over the method of procedure in that the ladies began to hold meetings of their own. The seventh day out, when the Misses Dryden and Sadtler passed one village they were besought to stop; they held some exercises and brought in a collection. They made a two miles' tour to Uppalapádu, conducted the Jubilee exercises and returned home with subscriptions of Rs. 27-4-6 ($13.63). Thereafter the ladies held separate meetings at Bukkapúram, Munangiváripálem Parchùr, Attôrta, Tumalúru, Adipalli, Repalli, Moparru, Jakkulaparemi and Kákumánu, and always with good results.

On the twelfth day out, after a compass of 105 miles through the Palnád Taluk, the party entered the Vinukonda Taluk, where the first meeting was held at Ipúru, a flourishing little congregation with a good school. Here the subscription amounted to Rs. 34-10-0 ($17.30).

On the fourteenth day out, after the camp had made about twenty-five miles of travel through the Vinukonda Taluk, we reached the Narasarowpett Taluk at Pariterlaváripálem. Here is a growing congregation and school, and the sum subscribed was Rs. 39-6-0 ($19.68). Owing to the distance to a number of important congregations in the Vinukonda Taluk, as well as in the Kanigiri Taluk of Nellore District (State), the inconvenience to so large a camping party forbade a Jubilee visit to those congregations, and they were regretfully omitted. In the Narasarowpett Taluk the party was compelled to divide up more and more and to allow but one of its number to visit any particular congregation, or otherwise many little flocks would be passed by. It had at the outset been intended to omit these smaller congregations and leave the teachers in charge to secure subscriptions, but it was becoming evident that such a method would be satisfactory neither to the people themselves nor successful. It was thus that on March 23d we had five meetings, including the main one, and on the 27th seven meetings were held. From this time on seldom less than six meetings were held daily, and the non-existence of congregations in any one vicinity became the sole occasion for the exception.

On the nineteenth day out, after a trip for the camp of forty-eight miles, through Narasarowpett Taluk, but with flank movements of hundreds of miles, the border of the Bapatla Taluk was reached near Timmarajapálem, when larger congregations and larger subscriptions became the order of the day. At this place the subscriptions were Rs. 127-4-0 ($63.62).

This nineteenth day of the tour was also remarkable for the total subscription being much larger than that of any previous twenty-four hours. Taking a bird's eye view of the whole tour we here group together some of the largest day's subscriptions thus begun on March 27th:

March 30th, two villages, Rs. 250	April 9th, eight villages, Rs. 323
July 27th, two villages, " 277	" 15th, six villages, " 323
" 26th, six villages, " 279	July 28th, two villages, " 357
" 23d, five villages, " 287	April 14th, seven villages, " 367
March 27th, six villages, " 289	March 28th, seven villages, " 431

Thus, as the work went on the results far exceeded our expectations.

On the 21st day out, and after a return from Perála and Chirála near the sea, it was evident that one of the servants was attacked by cholera. With a few exceptions, the health of all the party had been good, but this case in the camp at Káremchedu was a sad one. All night of March 29th remedies were used and stimulants administered, but grave uncertainty surrounded the case, and before the second nightfall the faithful fellow had passed away and was buried by members of the camp. Thus was the festival kept in the death of one of the party, and while some had given money and others toil, this man gave his life to the Jubilee.

On the twenty-second day of the tour there were two new items of interest. Word as to the nature of the Jubilee exercises and as to what the people were expected to do began to be noised about everywhere. A friendly rivalry sprang up among the better congregations, and the first to manifest this spirit was Kúnkalamiru, which had been for even three years without its own sub-catechist, school and house of worship. The gifts of this congregation went with a leap far above those previously given by any other, challenging the best congregations to do their utmost. A list of all congregations for the whole tour giving Rs. 150 and upwards is herewith appended:

Balasapádu . . . . Rs. 150	Vellúrti, two efforts . . . Rs. 172
Kollúru . . . . " 155	Kunkalamiru . . . . . . " 203
Mandúru . . . . " 165	Pámulapádu, two efforts . " 223
Káremchedu . . . . " 163	Rayapúdi, two efforts . . . " 235
Ipúru, two efforts . . . . " 166	

These were the most encouraging features among the many met with in this Jubilee.

The other feature brought out at Kunkalamiru was the erection of a large pavilion in which to hold the exercises. With timbers from their houses and timber from their employers, with mats from their sheds, sheets from their cots and colored clothes from their own persons, they had improvised a shed which was a comfort from the sun, cheerful in its colors and ample enough to accommodate the three hundred and more who had gathered together. Other places imitated the example thus set. In Répalli Taluk a neat pandal was erected at Duggirála, others were built at Yellavarru, Kuchepúdi Rèpalli and Yedlapalli, large ones were put up at Adepalli, the best one in design and ornament at Kollúru, while far exceeding all others in size, ornament, expense, comfort and number of mottoes were the two very large ones erected at Pálaparru and Uppalapádu, at each of which places a church dedication and a Jubilee celebration were held on the same day.

On the twenty-fifth day out, and after fifty-two miles for the main camp in a straight line through Bápatla Taluk, the party reached Duggirála in Répalli Taluk, where a small congregation, composed entirely of day laborers, gave Rs. 23-4-6 ($11.64) and from which place another and highly successful trip was entered upon. It was now April 7th, and all were called upon to endure bright suns and heated days. Zeal made endurable the heat and glare.

On the twenty-eighth day out began a new feature, that of escorts and music for the Jubilee party. At Koleparru these musicians escorted the party a full mile from the camp to the pavilion, marching through the town and gathering an ever-increasing mass of people as they went along. Escorts like this became common in Répalli Taluk and a few other places, while special mention must be made of Kollúru, Mandúru, Uppalapàdu, Pàlaparru, Gottapàdu, and Nevalikallu. At Gottapàdu, where the Christians are usually denied the liberty of the streets, in a crowd, it seemed, firstly, that every Christian man, woman and child had turned out in one grand procession, while, secondly, that the whole village portion had been struck with some earthquake and all the caste people tumbled out in wonderment to front doors and street sides. At Nevalikallu, at the breaking up of the camp, Christian and pagan, non-caste and caste, all united in the largest procession the town had ever seen to escort Dr. Unangst out of their village and on his way, after the usage for officials, rajahs and kings. More simple but yet more touching was the escort given Revs. Aberly and Uhl after the Jubilee at Rayapúdi, where, with banners and flags, the little folks led the way out through the town, chanting and singing as they went along.

On the thirtieth day out, and at a meeting at Béthapúdi, the Jubilee efforts made were seconded most heartily by Mr. Sebastian, Apothecary of Répalli at the time, as well as by his family; Mr. and Mrs. Sebastian themselves being children of a mission in Mysore. He took a deep interest in all the exercises, and contributed liberally to the "Memorial." In a letter afterwards to the "Christian Patriot" of Madras, this brother wrote as appreciative a letter of these Jubilee exercises and of mission work in general, as is possible to be written. The instance shows how in India, as everywhere, the intelligently devout Christian stands up for his cause in all places and is not drawn away from the Lord, whatever his surroundings may be.

On the thirty-fourth day out, and after a camp circuit of seventy-one miles, the party left Répalli Taluk. A second trip was made into the Bápatla Taluk, and into the Palnad, while even a third was taken into the Sattenapalli.

On the forty-sixth day out, and on the Palnad second trip, was encountered a heavy shower of rain, making travel almost impossible. Such showers came afterwards upon the party at Rayapúdi and at Nevalikallu. At nine o'clock on this forty-sixth evening, in the dark and the rain, at a snail's pace through the soaked earth, bringing in Dr. Unangst, the ladies, one camp set and the daily shifted articles, seven carts with double pairs of bullocks to each cart came in a long cavalcade over roadless, pathless ways a whole afternoon from Tangéda. That calvacade, with its grinding and pushing of clogged wheels, stands for a type of how the Jubilee tour was made under difficulties.

On the fiftieth day out was begun a visit through the Guntur Taluk, with meetings, at five places, resulting in a subscription of Rs. 133-8-6 ($66.76).

On the fifty-third day out, at Dharanakórta, beginning the third trip into Sattenapalli Taluk, there was a novel seating arrangement for the people. The exercises were in a grove, and the teachers and catechist, moved by an original idea, had placed boards on pegs driven into the earth under the ends of each board, the whole forming three sides of a rectangle, and so new was the plan that the people at first passed the seats by and sat as usual upon the ground. Here many clowns and performers from the native festival just going on were present. These coming in their masks and painted bodies soon ceased to carry on their tricks and exhibitions, and sat down quite tamely to see and to listen.

On the fifty-fifth day out, the then only two horsemen of the camp had a remarkable ride of forty long miles, held meetings at four places and returned to camp at midnight, losing their way in the darkness on the return.

On July 31st, and in accordance with the general plan, the closing Jubilee exercises were held in the new and spacious College Hall at Guntur. Here the events of the tour were reviewed and additional subscriptions of Rs. 615 ($307.50) were secured. The figures here represented show the magnitude of the work accomplished. The days in camp were fifty-nine, from March 4th to July 30th; in Vinukónda Taluk, six; in Bápatla, twenty-nine; in Narasarowpett, thirty-one; in Palnad, thirty-seven; in Répalli, forty-three, and in Sattenapalli forty-six places were visited, making a total of 192; subscriptions were received from 223 places, and the total pledged was made that day to reach Rs. 14,348-14-8 ($7,174.44). This sum has since been increased so as to make the handsome total of Rs. 15,265-1-8 ($7,632.55) from 227 places.

It is still a question as to how faithful the people will be in paying the money subscribed. Doubtless some of the subscriptions will never be made good. Eighteen months and two years have been given as the limits within which the money should be paid; five months of this period have now elapsed at this writing, March, 1894, and the sum already paid into the treasurer's hand is Rs. 3,211-13-2 ($1,605.91). This is assuring, to say the least.

The Jubillee tour, its exercises and subscriptions, brought out into prominence the condition of the mission at the close of its first fifty years. But for this tour neither missionaries nor people would have known the varied features and vast extent of the work. The simple statements brought to every one's understanding, that 20,000 Christians had been received into the mission, of whom 14,265 were now living and faithful, and that these Christians lived in 425 villages, made a great impression upon the Church. The tour has created favorable impressions and raised new questions in the minds of thousands of caste people, it has brought the yet pagan portion of the "depressed classes" into closer contact with Christianity; it has given strength to the Christian community as well as new ideas and plans of work, it has vastly encouraged the missionaries, it will cheer the whole Lutheran Church, and it will speak out to all the world for all time, how despised and oppressed classes of pagan people have been elevated to a certain extent, brought into some self-respect, and made capable of extensive efforts in Christian work, through the gospel of the Son of God. From this outlook it can be nothing but cheering, notwithstanding all stumbling and falling out by the way, to go on into the work of the *next fifty years*.

APPENDIX II.

RULES OF THE AMERICAN EVANGELICAL LUTHERAN MISSION.

I. DIVISION OF LABOR, HEADQUARTERS AND APPOINTMENTS.

1. All division of labor shall be subject to the decision of Conference.

2. The headquarters of all new divisions of the mission district shall be sanctioned by Conference.

3. All appointments of unordained mission workers shall be made by Conference.

II. QUALIFICATIONS AND PROMOTION OF MISSION WORKERS.

1. All unordained workers shall be confirmed in mission work only on condition that they are free from all objectionable caste prejudice, and possess the requisite intellectual and moral qualifications.

2. All promotions of unordained workers shall be made by Conference after an examination in experience, intellectual attainments and moral conduct.

3. A candidate for a sub-pastor's appointment shall have a certificate of having acquitted himself well for one or two years as a matriculate or F. A. student of the A. E. L. M. College, Guntur, or of having passed a prescribed examination, and shall also have experience as a gospel worker in the mission.

4. A sub-pastor may be licensed as a minister of the gospel, pending a prescribed examination, or on condition of passing such examination.

5. Any worker shall be refused work by the mission who does not agree to go where the mission sends him, unless he can give satisfactory reasons why he should not go.

6. Work shall not be given in our mission to any one who has left us as a baptized member of the Church, and been immersed by the Baptists.

7. Work shall not be given to any one who is not willing to maintain the Lutheran mode of baptism as in accordance with Scripture.

8. Work shall not be given to any one from another mission who does not bring a satisfactory testimonial of character and qualifications

from his mission, and who has not been subject to an examination by the missionary who intends to employ him.

9. No one shall be admitted to regular gospel work in our mission, unless he or she be a communicant member of our church.

III. EXAMINATION.

1. All unordained workers shall be examined only in the classes to which they belong.

2. All unordained workers who are under forty years of age shall be required to appear at the annual examination. The attendance of all over forty years of age, and of helpers and school teachers, shall be optional.

3. The examinees who fail to obtain twenty-five per cent. of answers at the annual examination, including optional candidates who receive batta, and those who are absent without a providential reason, shall pay a monthly fine into the mission treasury for twelve months, beginning with the first month after the examination, as follows:

2d class catechists	Rs.	1 0 0
1st " "	"	0 12 0
4th " sub-catechists	"	0 10 0
3d " "	"	0 8 0
2d " "	"	0 6 0
1st " "	"	0 4 0
Helpers and school teachers	"	0 2 0

IV. SALARIES.

1. The salary of a native pastor shall in each case be determined by Conference.

2. Three grades of sub-pastors shall be appointed and designated for work, the monthly salary of each to be as follows:

1st grade	Rs.	12
2d "	"	15
3d "	"	18

Subsequent promotions are to be determined by Conference.

3. The scale of monthly salaries for unordained workers, besides the sub-pastors, shall be as follows:

2d class catechists	Rs.	10
1st " "	"	9
4th " sub-catechists	"	8
3d " "	"	7
2d " "	"	6
1st " "	"	5
2d " helpers	"	4
1st " "	"	3

4. The salaries of the wives and children of mission workers who teach school, shall be as follows, and shall be considered half salary:

For a school of from 8 to 12 regular pupils, Rs. 1–8–0 for the 1st standard.

For a school of from 13 to 16 regular pupils, Rs. 2–0–0 for the 1st standard.

For a school above 16 regular pupils, Rs. 2–8–0 for the 1st standard, and annas 8 for each standard above the first.

5. The salaries of other school teachers shall be as follows, and shall be considered half salary up to and including the 3d standard, after which the salary shall be considered full salary:

For a 1st standard school of not less than 8 regular pupils, Rs. 3–0–0
" 2d " " " 12 " " " 3–8–0
" 3d " " " 16 " " " 4–0–0
" 4th " " " 20 " " " 5–0–0

6. No increase of salary shall be paid for any standard after the first, which has less than three pupils.

7. All government grants to the village schools shall be given to the teachers of said schools who get half salary, and half said grants to those who get full salary.

8. The monthly salary for keeping the Reading Room and Book Depot shall be Rs. 5 and one-sixteenth of all sales of books, tracts and stationery effected by the keeper. Issues shall not be subject to a commission.

9. The monthly salary of a missionary's munshi shall be as follows: For a daily service of one hour, first year, Rs. 5; second year, Rs. 6.
" " two hours, " " 7; " " 8.
" " three hours, " " 9; " " 10.

V. BATTA, TRANSFER, POSTAGE, PUPILS' FEES.

1. No batta for dieting or other purposes shall be given to mission workers, except by special sanction of Conference.

2. Village school teachers shall be moved from place to place at the expense of the schools or patrons whom they serve.

3. Unordained mission workers transferred from one sub-division to another at their own request, or for a fault, shall defray their own travelling expenses, otherwise the mission shall pay their travelling expenses at a rate not exceeding two annas a mile.

4. Medical expenses on behalf of all our native workers shall be borne by the patients themselves, unless otherwise specially provided for by Conference.

5. Postage on all *bona fide* mission mail matter shall be paid by the mission.

6. No fees shall be paid to pupils for attending school.

VI. Rules Concerning Leave for Sickness and Other Causes.

1. All days of sickness on the part of our mission workers shall be reported at the monthly meetings, or at regular intervals, to the missionary or pastor in charge, who shall have the same recorded in a book kept for the purpose in the President's office, showing names of the sick, date and kind of sickness.

2. Full pay shall be allowed for thirty days' sickness per annum, and half pay for one month only in excess of that period.

3. Cases of ordained native pastors coming under this rule shall be disposed of by special consideration of Conference.

4. Pastors and sub-pastors having supervision of mission work, shall report to Conference monthly or at regular intervals, the number of days of sickness, names and kind of sickness of mission workers who are under their supervision.

5. A missionary or pastor in charge may give casual leave in cases of emergency, or on important private affairs to mission workers under him for a term which shall not exceed fifteen days at a time.

6. All such casual leave shall not exceed thirty days per annum, except it be on the loss of full pay.

7. Sub-pastors and catechists may take for themselves or give to mission workers under them, casual leave not exceeding four days at a time, otherwise the approval of the missionary or pastor in charge must be obtained.

8. The time spent by unordained mission workers at their residence outside of their field of work, shall be placed to their casual or sick leave account, as the case may be.

9. Pastors and sub-pastors shall report all cases of casual leave to Conference, and shall have the same recorded in a book kept for that purpose, giving names of persons, date, extent and object of leave.

10. Any act of fraud or deception committed in respect of these or any of these rules shall be reported without delay to Conference, who shall inflict such punishment on the offender as the nature of the case may require.

VII. Village Schools, and School Teachers' Duties.

1. Pupils who are less than four or more than twenty-one years of age are excluded.

2. The Ten Commandments, Creed, Monthly Verses, First Catechism and Lord's Prayer shall be taught in all our mission village schools.

3. Pupils shall not be promoted beyond the standard in which they have not passed the necessary examination.

4. Those who have attended school less than half the number of school days, shall not be considered regular pupils.

5. Only such as are more than sixteen years of age may be appointed school teachers, and if they are Christians, they shall be communicants.

6. Only those who have passed the required examination or have the necessary qualification, may teach the higher standards in our Mission Result Grant Schools.

7. Any teacher failing to observe these or any of these rules, shall be punished.

VIII. DUTIES OF SUB-PASTORS.

1. Sub-pastors must be free from caste prejudice and preach the Word of God to all classes of people.

2. It shall be their duty to have the general oversight of any part of the mission field assigned to them by Conference.

3. It shall be their duty to examine the reports of catechists, sub-catechists, school teachers, and other mission workers and report to the pastor or missionary in charge.

4. They shall prepare and report correct statements of salary and other accounts of unordained mission workers.

5. They shall act for the pastor in case of the latter's absence on leave, or otherwise, ministerial acts excepted.

6. They shall assist the pastor, or missionary, in such other mission work as may be necessary.

7. They shall rule well their own families, and thus set a good example to their neighbors.

IX. DUTIES OF CATECHISTS.

I. The catechists shall report every month as follows:

1. Number of members attending church in each congregation.

2. Number of men, women, boys and girls that learn the catechism, monthly verses and other subjects.

3. What and how much they have learned.

4. Number and names of congregations visited.

5. Number and names of villages visited.

6. Time spent with each congregation and at each village visited.

7. Texts and subjects of sermons, where preached, and talks with the heathen.

8. Objections and other principal remarks of the heathen and answers given them.

9. Number of regular services and prayer meetings, and where held.
10. Number of candidates for baptism.
11. Amount contributed by each congregation.
12. Examination of all the mission schools in their respective divisions and the result.
13. Examining, signing and particulars of each sub-catechist's diary at the time of visiting.
14. Cases inquired into and settled.
15. The date of the visits made and the work done.
16. The state of health of each village visited.
17. The general condition of each congregation and school visited.
18. Name, age, and sex of members who have died.
19. Number of days at home and at work.

II. The catechists shall spend twenty days each month on circuit, including the time required to report.

III. The catechists who neglect to perform these duties shall be subject to a fine.

X. DUTIES OF SUB-CATECHISTS.

I. Sub-catechists shall report every month as follows.

1. Number of men, women, boys and girls attending church in each congregation.
2. Number of men, women, boys and girls that learn the catechism, monthly verses, and other subjects.
3. What and how much they have learned.
4. Number of visits to all congregations in their respective sub-divisions.
5. The date of each visit, of the Catechist's visit and of the visits of others.
6. Number of villages visited and their names.
7. Number of Christian boys and girls who are more than four years of age.
8. Number of Christian boys and girls who attend school.
9. Number of regular services and prayer meetings held and names of the villages where held.
10. Number of new inquirers, men, women and children.
11. Name and contribution of each member.
12. Number of days and nights absent on duty.
13. Number of days work and the kind of work with the congregation at home.
14. Time spent in work each day.
15. Efforts made to induce children to attend school.

II. The sub-catechists shall spend an equitable number of days and nights every month with each congregation in their respective subdivisions without neglecting neighboring heathen villages.

III. The sub-pastors and catechists shall have the sub-catechists read their (sub-catechists) diaries before the congregations among whom they work.

IV. Those who do not work according to these rules shall be subject to a fine.

XI. MONTHLY MEETINGS AND REPORT OF MISSION RECEIPTS.

1. The unordained workers of the mission shall have their monthly meetings at the headquarters of the minister in charge for the purpose of reporting their work.

2. At each headquarters when the mission workers meet to report their work and receive their salaries, a half day at each monthly meeting shall be devoted to public exercises, presided over by the missionary or pastor in charge, consisting of:

a. Devotional exercises.
b. Reading of sub-pastors' and catechists' diaries.
c. Short speeches on practical subjects.
d. Criticisms on the diaries read and suggestions for improvement.

3. All mission workers shall report to Conference all moneys received on account of mission work.

4. Careful estimates shall be made of all the work done by the people in the congregations, and of all help given in cash or otherwise, for our annual reports, and the reports of the same shall be made to Conference.

5. For each absence from the monthly report meetings without a providential reason or leave, a fine shall be collected as follows:

For each pastor . . . . Rs. 0 8 0
" sub-pastor . . . . " 0 4 0
" catechist . . . . " 0 2 0
For others . . . . " 0 1 0

XII. BOARDERS.

I. Admission of Boarders.

1. New boarders shall be admitted only by order of Conference, and shall be maintained for one year before being recommended for patrons.

2. Boarders offered to be supported by outside parties shall not be received without the sanction of Conference.

3. The marriage engagements of our mission boarding boys shall be subject to the approval of Conference on pain of a fine of Rs. 10, and applicants whose marriage engagements have been previously made, shall be subject to special consideration.

4. No boy shall be admitted into the boarding establishment unless he has passed the second standard.

5. No boys shall be admitted unless they are baptized, and unless they themselves or their parents or guardians are communicants.

6. As far as practicable, all boarding boys shall be admitted at the beginning of the Guntur school year.

7. No married persons shall be received into our boarding school.

II. Allowances, fees, etc.

1. The boarding boys shall be allowed only such plain food and clothing as they will have to be accustomed to in the villages.

2. Rich parents, or those who have adequate means, shall be required to contribute towards the support of their children in our boarding establishment.

3. The minimum monthly payments to be made by parents or guardians, whose children are admitted into the boarding establishment, shall be on the following scale:

Pastors and all others receiving like salary	Rs.	1 8 0
Sub-pastors " " "	"	0 12 0
Catechists " " "	"	0 8 0
Sub-catechists, 4th and 3d class, and all others receiving like salary	"	0 6 0
Sub-catechists, 2d and 1st class, and all others receiving like salary	"	0 4 0
Helpers, school teachers and all others receiving like salary.	"	0 2 0

4. All guardians or parents who receive a salary of Rs. 6 per month and upwards shall be required to furnish all needed clothes for their children in school.

5. All other parents or guardians shall be required to furnish needed clothes for their children, except as follows:

(*a*) Pupils of the 1st, 2d and 3d forms of the high school will be furnished two suits of unbleached long cloth annually, *viz*., one pancha and one coat after the Christmas vacation, and one each of the same after the May vacation.

(*b*) Pupils of the 4th, 5th and 6th forms, high school, will be furnished with two suits of bleached long cloth annually, *viz*., one pancha and one coat after the Christmas vacation, and one each of the same after the May vacation.

(*c*) Orphans in all classes up to and including the 3d form will be given two caps and one turban each, of a cheap kind, annually. Orphans in classes of the branch school and 1st form high school shall be given four upper and four lower cloths of unbleached long cloth, and orphans in the other classes will be furnished with four suits corresponding to the kind given other boarders of those classes.

APPENDIX. 311

III. Rules of conduct, etc.

Boarders are required to observe the following rules:

1. To rise not later than 5:30 or 6 o'clock a. m.; to wash their faces, necks and hands; comb their heads; put away their bedding; dress and appear before the Missionary or person in charge, for inspection, not later than half an hour after rising.

2. To take their morning meal immediately after inspection and prepare for school.

3. To take their noon meal not later than one o'clock p. m. and their evening meal between 7 and 8 p. m.

4. To present their cooking utensils and all vessels and furniture in their charge for inspection whenever required.

5. To bathe every day, if possible.

6. To leap or white-wash their houses at such times as Conference or the Superintendent may order.

7. To remove all nuisances committed in the vicinity of their houses.

8. To allow no cattle, horses or hogs to be kept or tied inside, or in front of their houses.

9. To entertain no visitor or relative without the special permission of the Missionary or person in charge, and to allow no loafer, or beggar of any kind, to stop at their dwellings.

10. To spend a portion of their time in manual labor for their Mission.

11. To cultivate industrious habits both of mind and body.

12. To attend to private devotions immediately after rising in the morning and before retiring in the evening.

13. To wear no jewels or expensive clothing, such as shoulder cloths, etc,, and not to carry umbrellas without permission.

14. To abstain strictly from all use of snuff, tobacco, betel nut and alcoholic drinks.

15. To retire not later than 10 p. m. and put out lights at that time except by special permission.

16. To march to church, prayer and other meetings, and to school, in ranks.

17. To obtain permission from the manager to go to the bazaar, reading room hospital and dresser's house, or to obtain the same from the missionary in charge to go to all other places not attended in ranks, or to visit home.

18. To make no purchases in the bazaar on Sunday.

19. To obtain sick leave from the missionary in charge in order to remain home from school.

20. To attend all meetings held for their improvement, all ap-

pointed recitations, all public religious services, and all other services appointed for them.

21. To submit to all punishments of the manager, not exceeding five strokes of the rattan for each punishment.

IV. Miscellaneous.

1. Half the cost of all non-school books, except the *Christian Guide*, must be paid by boarders desiring them.

2. A blank book shall be opened for all boarders who have read two years in our boarding-school, in which they shall be required to sign their names, promising to work in the mission, if work is offered them, for not less than 5 years, or else to refund the amount of support they shall have received in board, clothes, management and tuition, after that time in case they engage in other work.

3 All younger boarders who enter the 3d class shall be permitted, as a test, to study English one year.

V. Rules concerning boys on leaving school.

1. Boarding boys who leave the school before they have passed the 4th class shall be employed as helpers, and all boarders shall be required to pass the sub-catechists' examination before appointment to a sub-catechist or higher position.

2. Each boy who is selected and sent out to work by order of conference shall be given one box.

3. Pupils who study creditably in the 3d form shall be entitled to the salary of a 2d class sub-catechist on their passing the 1st class sub-catechists' examination. Pupils who study creditably in the 4th form shall be entitled to a 3d class sub catechist's salary on passing the examination for 2d class sub-catechists, and pupils who study creditably in the 5th and 6th forms shall be entitled to the 4th class sub-catechist's salary on passing the 3d class sub-catechist's examination.

XIII. Concerning Festivals.

1. The congregations of our mission shall abstain from all heathen and Muhammadan masquerades when observing the Christian Festivals, such as Christmas, Easter, etc.

2. The use of intoxicating liquors as a beverage on festive as well as on other occasions is strictly forbidden.

3. Processions with suitable Scripture mottoes, religious music and speeches on appropriate subjects are always proper on such occasions.

4. Participating in or assisting heathen and Muhammadan festivals is strictly forbidden.

5. The mission employees shall see that these rules are observed in our mission field.

6. Every violation of these or any of these rules shall subject the offender to a fine which may extend to rupees five for each offense.

XIV. Concerning Native Christian Marriages.

1. Half of all the marriage fees received by persons licensed in the mission to perform marriages shall be given to the conference, and all fees reported to conference.

2. All persons holding a license in our mission to solemnize marriages between native Christians shall, before solemnizing such marriages, ascertain the age of the parties to be married by referring to the record of baptisms in which the baptism of those to be married has been recorded, or, if such record is not accessible, by referring to the village Register of Births and Deaths.

3. A native Christian shall give notice of his intention to be married to any person licensed to solemnize marriages not less than ten days before the day on which he proposes to be married, and he shall not consult pancháugies of any caste as to any particular or propitious day for his marriage.

4. A violation of these or any of these rules shall render the offender liable to a fine of not less than Rs. 2, which may extend to Rs. 25.

XV. Prayer and School-Houses.

1. For a thatched-roof prayer house the mission will furnish materials and carpenter hire, the cost of the same not to exceed Rs. 50, and will furnish half the excess of this amount.

2. The mission will furnish the materials for a tile-roof prayer house, the total cost of which is not to exceed Rs. 100.

3. For all houses the total cost of which is more than Rs. 100, and not more than Rs. 300, the mission will furnish two-thirds of the total cost.

4. For all houses the total cost of which is in excess of Rs. 300, the mission will pay one-half the excess.

5. The grant of materials and other aid for the construction of prayer or school-houses shall be made by the mission to such congregations only as observe the Sabbath, and attend public worship regularly.

6. The congregations shall pay the cost of all repairs, if possible.

XVI. Support of the Helpless Poor.

1. The congregations throughout the mission are expected to assume the care and support of the helpless poor belonging to them.

XVII. Signature of Government Papers.

1. All the managers of schools under the mission shall be required to sign all public government papers for their schools by adding after the word "manager" "on behalf of the A. E. Mission."

XVIII. DRESS OF PASTORS AND SUB-PASTORS.

1. Our native pastors and sub-pastors, when performing ministerial or pulpit work, shall be required to wear a long black coat with suitable lower dress.

XIX. PROCEEDINGS AGAINST MISSION WORKERS.

1. In all cases of immorality reported against our mission workers, written statements and decisions must be given by Church Panchayats or the pastor.

INDEX.

A.

Aberly, 147. In charge of Theological Department, 245.
Albrecht, 151.
American Board, union with discontinued, 32.
Anglo-Vernacular Schools, 236. Government Grant to, 237.
Appendix I., Jubilee Tour, 293. II., Rules of the Mission, 303.
Arthur G. Watts Memorial College Building, Work of Dr. Uhl, 244. Gift of the Messrs. Watts and Indian Government, 245.

B.

Bapatla Taluk, 66. Palmyra Grove, 68. Principal towns of, 69.
Baptists, American, 42. Canadian, 44.
Boarding School, 184, 225. Ground for, 225. Boys and Girls, 226. Difficulties, 228. Growth of, 230.

C.

Caste prejudices, 240. Giving way, 241.
Central Authority, 259.
Church Mission Society, commenced, 43.
College, 231. Leavening influence of, 234. Results, 241. Curriculum, 242. Religious instruction, 242. Memorial Building, 243. Theological Department of, 245. Ground broken, corner-stone laid and opening, 245.
Congregational or mixed schools, 219. Benefits of, 221. Growth of, 223.
Cutter, 118.

D.

Dryden, Miss Fannie M., 159.
Duff, Dr., 232.

E.

Educational Work, 203. Higher Education, 205, 233. Policy of English Government, 207. Views of Dr. Miller, 210. Divisions of, 211. Girls' Schools, 211. Mixed or Congregational Schools, 219. Boarding Schools, 225. Difficulties, 228. Benefits, 241.
English Government, educational policy of, 207.
Evangelization, 252. Bazar and Village Preaching, 253. Colporteurage, 254. In the Palnad, 255. In Guntur, 256.

F.

Field, division of, 184.
Foreign Missions, early movement, 28. First Organization, 29. German Society, 31.

G.

General Council, transfer of work, 74.
Girls' Schools, 211. Opposition to, 212. The first, 214. High caste, 216. Growth of, 217. Maintenance of, 218. Extent of work, 218.
Godavery Delta Mission, 43. District, 72.
Grant-in-Aid Code, 174.
Grönning, 111. Retired, 112.
Growth of Work, 275.
Guntur Taluk, 61. Evangelistic work in, 256.
Guntur Town, Government offices and business, 62, 63. Centre of Mission Work, and road centre, 63. Neighboring towns, 65. Work in, 184, 185.
Gunn, born, educated and sailed, 103. Health declined, 104. Death and character, 107.
Gutzlaff, 30.

H.

Harpster, 113.
Hay, 41.
Heise, 113.
Hermannsburg Mission, 44.
Heyer, offered himself, 32. Resigned, offered a second time and sailed, 33. Arrived in India, 44. An ideal missionary, 87. Birthplace, 87. Student and Home Missionary, 88. Appointed, 91. Sailed, 92. Arrived in India, 93. Arrived in Guntur, 94. First furlough, 95. Second visit to India, 96. Trip to Palnad, 96. Work in Palnad established, 97. Labors of, 98. Returns to America, and engages in Home Mission Work, 99. Third Visit to India, 100. Work at Rajahmundry, 101. Leaves India, death, 102.
High School and College and its Branches, 231.
Higher Education, 232, 233. Leavening influence, 234. Extent of work, 235.

I.

Increase, 275.
India Conference, 183. Central authority, 259. Wisdom of the plan, 259.
Inter-denominational comity, 288. Increasing confidence, 290–292.

J.

Jubilee Tour, 293. Program of, 294–296. Subscriptions taken, 299.

K.

Kistler, Miss S. R., 161.
Krishna District, location and division of, 45. Rank and population of, 47. Products and improvements, 48. Farming population, 49. Natural features and geological formation, 49. Government of, 50. Revenue and village life, 51. Judicial and police government, 52. Public works, 52. Salt and spirits, 53. Educational, 53. Table of area and population, 69. Occupations, 70.

Kugler, Miss Dr., 157. Opened dispensary, 158. At the World's Fair, 159.

L.

Long, 118. Death of, 120.

M.

Madras Presidency, 36.
Madras, City of, 38.
Marriages, early, 229.
Martz, 108. Term of service, 110.
Medical Work, 188. Value of, 189. Government Dispensaries and female medical missionaries, 191. Dispensary opened, 193. Hospital, endowed beds, 195.
Miller, Dr. Views of on higher education, 210.
Mission College, organized, 242.
Missionaries, larger force of, 290.
Mission Work, many-sided character, 250.

N.

Narasarowpet Taluk, 57. Legend, 57. History of, 59. Temple, 60.
Native Workers, Staff of, 164. Early helpers, 169. First report of, 170. Growth and grade of, 171. Variety of work, 260. Promotions, 264.
New Testament, first in Telugu, 40.
Nichols, 145. Death and Memorial of, 147.
Noble, converts under, 43.
North German Mission, 72.

O.

Oneness of the work, 266.
Old Problem, 272.
Old Testament, first in Telugu, 40.
Ordained native workers, 174, 175.

Organization, 181. Different departments, 186, 188. By Taluks, 257.
Our India Mission, Birth of, 94.

P.

Palnad Taluk, location and extent, 54. Evangelistic work in, 255.
Printing press, first, 31.
Preparation, work of, 270.
Primary education, importance of, 279.
Progress of the work, 269.
Propagation of the Gospel, Society for, 44.
Prospects, 288.
Protestant Missions, first, 40.

R.

Rajahmundry, transfer of mission, 72–79. Rev. Long's connection with, 76.
Repalli Taluk, soil and crops, 65. Canals and towns, 66.
Results, spiritual, 281, 282.
Rheinus, 30, 32. Appeal of, 90.
Roman Catholics, first in Telugu country, 39.
Rowe, 131. Superintendent Public Schools, 133. Originated Children's Missionary Societies and sailed for India, 134. Training School, 135. Furlough, 136. Returned to India, death, 137. Character, 138.

S.

Sadtler, Miss Amy L., 163.
Samaldas Agraharam School, 216.
Satenapalli Taluk, 60. Interesting places and discoveries, 60.
Schmidt, 73, 101.
Schmucker, 90.
Schnure, 140.
Self-government, 177–180, 263, 284.
Self-support, 262. Growth in, 283. Proportion contributed, 284.
Snyder, 114. Death of, 116.

Staff of workers, early, 80. List of, up to 1894, 82–86.
Stokes, 93.
Swartz, 144.

T.

Taluks, organized work in, 257, 258.
Telugu, dialect, 36. Old and New Testament in, 40.
Theological School, 245. Course of study, 247. Aims, 247. Sunday-school and Bible classes in, 247.

U.

Uhl, 129–131. Account of Jubilee Tour, 293.
Unangst, only man in field, 74. Sketch of, 122–126.

V.

Vinukonda Taluk, 55. Geology of, 56.

W.

Wives of Missionaries, 153.
Wolf, 142.
Woman's Work, organized, 154, 185.

Y.

Yeiser, 151.

Z.

Zenana Work, 196. Begun, 200. Home Classes opened, 201.

www.ingramcontent.com/pod-product-compliance
Lightning Source LLC
Chambersburg PA
CBHW022020240426
43667CB00042B/1005